★ The American Novel ★

GENERAL EDITOR

Emory Elliott
University of California, Riverside

New Essays on
Sister Carrie

Edited by

Donald Pizer

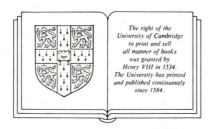

The right of the
University of Cambridge
to print and sell
all manner of books
was granted by
Henry VIII in 1534.
The University has printed
and published continuously
since 1584.

CAMBRIDGE UNIVERSITY PRESS

Cambridge

New York   Port Chester   Melbourne   Sydney

Published by the Press Syndicate of the University of Cambridge
The Pitt Building, Trumpington Street, Cambridge CB2 1RP
40 West 20th Street, New York, NY 10011, USA
10 Stamford Road, Oakleigh, Melbourne 3166, Australia

First published 1991

Printed in the United States of America

Library of Congress Cataloging-in-Publication Data

New essays on Sister Carrie / edited by Donald Pizer.
p. cm. – (The American novel)
Includes bibliographical references.
ISBN 0-521-38278-5 (hardcover). – ISBN 0-521-38714-0 (pbk.)
1. Dreiser, Theodore, 1871–1945. Sister Carrie. I. Pizer,
Donald. II. Series.
PS3507.R55S59 1991
813'.52 – dc20   91-2609

British Library Cataloguing in Publication Data

New essays on Sister Carrie. – (The American Novel)
1. United States 2. Dreiser, Theodore, *1871–1945*
I. Pizer, Donald II. Series
813.52

ISBN 0–521–38278–5 hardback
ISBN 0–521–38714–0 paperback

Contents

Contents

4
Sister Carrie: The City, the Self,
and the Modes of Narrative Discourse

Series Editor's Preface

In literary criticism the last twenty-five years have been particularly fruitful. Since the rise of the New Criticism in the 1950s, which focused attention of critics and readers upon the text itself – apart from history, biography, and society – there has emerged a wide variety of critical methods which have brought to literary works a rich diversity of perspectives: social, historical, political, psychological, economic, ideological, and philosophical. While attention to the text itself, as taught by the New Critics, remains at the core of contemporary interpretation, the widely shared assumption that works of art generate many different kinds of interpretation has opened up possibilities for new readings and new meanings.

Before this critical revolution, many American novels had come to be taken for granted by earlier generations of readers as having an established set of recognized interpretations. There was a sense among many students that the canon was established and that the larger thematic and interpretative issues had been decided. The task of the new reader was to examine the ways in which elements such as structure, style, and imagery contributed to each novel's acknowledged purpose. But recent criticism has brought these old assumptions into question and has thereby generated a wide variety of original, and often quite surprising, interpretations of the classics, as well as of rediscovered novels such as Kate Chopin's *The Awakening*, which has only recently entered the canon of works that scholars and critics study and that teachers assign their students.

The aim of The American Novel Series is to provide students of American literature and culture with introductory critical guides to

American novels now widely read and studied. Each volume is devoted to a single novel and begins with an introduction by the volume editor, a distinguished authority on the text. The introduction presents details of the novel's composition, publication history, and contemporary reception, as well as a survey of the major critical trends and readings from first publication to the present. This overview is followed by four or five original essays, specifically commissioned from senior scholars of established reputation and from outstanding younger critics. Each essay presents a distinct point of view, and together they constitute a forum of interpretative methods and of the best contemporary ideas on each text.

It is our hope that these volumes will convey the vitality of current critical work in American literature, generate new insights and excitement for students of the American novel, and inspire new respect for and new perspectives upon these major literary texts.

Emory Elliott
University of California, Riverside

Note on the Text

Sister Carrie was published by Doubleday, Page and Company of New York in early November 1900. In later years, Dreiser made only one change in the text of the novel, in 1907, when he revised a passage in Chapter 1 describing Drouet. Several reviewers of the first edition had noted Dreiser's verbatim use in the passage of a portion of one of George Ade's sketches in *Fables in Slang* (1899), and Dreiser was undoubtedly sensitive to the charge of plagiarism. The 1907 revised text served as the text for many later reprintings of *Sister Carrie*, including the popular Modern Library edition of 1932 and the frequent paperback reprints of the novel since the 1950s. In 1981, however, the University of Pennsylvania Press published an edition of *Sister Carrie* based not on Dreiser's 1907 revision of the Doubleday, Page edition but on his handwritten first draft of the novel, a draft which contains many passages later cut by Dreiser and his friend Arthur Henry as well as a different ending. Although the editors of the Pennsylvania Edition claimed that Dreiser's cuts and revisions constitute his self-censorship of the novel in order to assure its publication and that the handwritten draft is therefore the superior work, these claims have met with serious objections, and many scholars have preferred to maintain the revised text of 1907 as the principal text of the novel. The essays in this volume therefore rely primarily on the Norton Critical Edition of *Sister Carrie*, edited by Donald Pizer (New York: Norton, 1970; 2nd ed., 1991), an edition which is based on Dreiser's 1907 revision of the Doubleday, Page edition. However, all students of Dreiser have also acknowledged the importance of the Pennsylvania Edition in making available for critical use Dreiser's uncut prepublication version of the novel. Thus, several of the essays in this volume rely occasionally on the Pennsylvania Edition for specific passages not in the Norton Edition; and the essay by Thomas P. Riggio, because of its dependence on the fuller portrayal of Carrie in the Pennsylvania Edition, cites that text primarily. Except for Riggio's essay, therefore, page references to *Sister Carrie* which appear in parentheses after quotations are to the Norton Critical Edition; page references to the novel which refer to the Pennsylvania Edition have "Penn" immediately following the page number. For Riggio's essay, page references in parentheses are to the Pennsylvania Edition; references to the Norton Edition are followed by an "N" within the parentheses.

1

Introduction

DONALD PIZER

SISTER CARRIE, like *Madame Bovary* and *The Waste Land*, is both a major work of art and an important landmark in the development of literary modernism. A distinctive characteristic of works of this kind is their centrality in efforts to define the nature of modern thought and expression. Almost always controversial and even held in contempt at their appearance, such works have continued to stimulate critical anxiety right up to the present. What is the new sensibility here expressed, it is asked, and how can our understanding of this sensibility aid our understanding of the intellectual and cultural space we continue to occupy? Unlike Flaubert's masterpiece of irony and Eliot's great symbolic poem, *Sister Carrie* also raises important questions about the very nature of significant art. How can a novel seemingly so unconsciously shaped and so inept in its devices and language hold generation after generation of sophisticated readers? It is at the complex inter-section of these two lines of inquiry – *Sister Carrie* as a novel which achieves its penetrating insight into our lives almost in spite of itself – that much criticism of the work has both flourished and floundered.

Theodore Dreiser's life and career from his birth in 1870 to the appearance of *Sister Carrie* in 1900 are intimately related both to the depth and to the awkwardness of the novel.[1] Dreiser's father was a German Catholic immigrant, his mother of Pennsylvania Mennonite farm background, and the family large and poor. Other American writers had grown up in limited circumstances, but no major American author before Dreiser participated so fully in the new industrial and urban world of America in the late nineteenth century – a world in which hosts of immigrant poor struggled to

1

gain a foothold in the vast sprawl of an emerging metropolis. This had not been the principal fact of the youth of William Dean Howells, Mark Twain, or Henry James, the major writers of the generation just prior to Dreiser's, nor was it that of Stephen Crane or Frank Norris, Dreiser's foremost contemporaries, even though they wrote about the new urban life of their time. It was Dreiser alone who had been hustled as a child from one small Indiana town to the next while his father struggled to make a living and who as an adolescent and again as a young man had been plunged into the hurly-burly of Chicago and had precariously held on there as dishwasher, stove cleaner, freight car tracer, warehouse clerk, and laundry truck driver until finally, in early 1892, he broke into newspaper work as a reporter for the Chicago *Globe*.

During the next eight years Dreiser, by dint of hard work and a tenacious will, carved out a career for himself in journalism. By early 1894 he was a successful reporter for the St. Louis *Republic* and was on the verge of marrying a local schoolteacher of good family. But, like Carrie herself, he restlessly wanted something vaguely "higher" or "better" than this fate and so pushed on until, after short stays in Toledo and Pittsburgh, he landed, in late 1894, in New York. There, after some struggle, and at a point much like the down-and-out stage of Hurstwood's New York career, he managed to push his way to the top of the highly competitive popular journalism world of the 1890s – first as editor of *Ev'ry Month*, a magazine devoted largely to the publication of sheet music, and then as a free-lance contributor to the many new ten-cent magazines which had sprung up in the 1890s. From late 1897 to late 1899, when he began *Sister Carrie*, Dreiser ground out over 100 articles on such subjects as "Haunts of Nathaniel Hawthorne," "The Chicago Drainage Canal," and "Women Who Have Won Distinction in Music," becoming a leader in the field.

So this was the Dreiser who in October 1899 sat down to write *Sister Carrie*. He had experienced – as he later recorded in his remarkable autobiographies *Dawn* (1931) and *Newspaper Days* (1922) – the rough edges of life as had few American authors. He had also known, in his own life and in those of his brothers and sisters, the core of hope and expectation – usually thwarted but occasionally fulfilled – seemingly inherent in the American experience. As a writer, he had developed a journalistic facility, but since he had not yet attempted to write about life as he knew it, he had seldom expressed himself beyond the conventions of the newspaper report and the magazine article. (Almost all of Dreiser's creative work up to the summer before he began *Sister Carrie* had consisted of lachrymose magazine verse.) He came to the writing of *Sister Carrie*, in other words, intending to say something true and resonant about the new American experience he had encountered at first hand, but he also came with only a half-formed sense of how to do so. The novels of Balzac and Hardy, two of his early enthusiasms, had revealed to him that the modern novel could deal profoundly and movingly with the conditions of modern life by depicting the lives of common people. But aside from these rough guides he had to find his own way.

This process had begun in the summer of 1899. Dreiser had again reached a plateau in his career and again, like the ever-rocking Carrie, had become restless. Recently married to Sara White (also called Sallie or Jug), the conventional-minded Missouri schoolteacher he had been engaged to for over four years, he was also at the height of his success as a popular journalist. From this resting place of stability and achievement Dreiser was pushed into the hazardous waters of fiction by his friend Arthur Henry. He had met Henry in the spring of 1894, when Henry – then an editor of the Toledo *Blade* – had employed him briefly during the time when Dreiser was gradually making his way toward New York. The two men immediately became friends. Although Henry was never to write anything of importance, and although his ideas never extended beyond the obvious, he shared with Dreiser at this point in Dreiser's career a romantic enthusiasm for the possibilities of life and, more specifically, for their own possibilities as writers. So when Henry turned up in New York in the summer of 1897, himself somewhat adrift, the two renewed their friendship, and Henry invited Dreiser to join him at his home on the Maumee River, near Toledo. But Dreiser, who at this point was just beginning his free-lance career after two years of editing *Ev'ry Month*, could not take up the invitation until the summer of 1899. Then, accompanied by Jug, he spent over two months on the Maumee with Henry and his wife.

It was in this setting, and at this moment of equilibrium, that Dreiser, encouraged by Henry, made his first full-scale effort to write fiction. He had attempted a few imitative stories during his early days in New York, and he had written a number of minor semifictional sketches while editing *Ev'ry Month*. But now, at twenty-eight, he made a concerted effort for the first time. The four stories that he wrote that summer, all of which were published in 1901 and later collected in *Free and Other Stories* (1918), differ widely in subject matter and theme. But all contain themes which were to preoccupy Dreiser not only in his early novels but throughout his career. It was as though the act of turning to fiction had suddenly crystallized his essential response to life as his other authorial roles — reporter, editorial writer, poet, popular journalist — had not. Perhaps the most significant of these stories were "McEwen of the Shining Slave Makers" and "Nigger Jeff." Both are personal allegories, in the same way that the careers of Carrie and Hurstwood represent some of Dreiser's deepest feelings about himself. In both stories, a detached observer — McEwen watching groups of warring ants at his feet, the young newspaperman Davies sent to report a rape case and its aftermath — is plunged into the turmoil of powerful feelings and violent action that he has been observing and so acquires a recognition of the tragic center of life. This core of emotion and struggle, Dreiser appears to be saying, must be understood if life at its deepest level is to be understood, and it is the function of the writer to force the reader — as McEwen and Davies have been forced — into an acceptance of this truth. "I'll get it all in," Davies cries at the end of "Nigger Jeff," after having seen and responded to the powerful feelings preceding and following Jeff's lynching. And this no doubt was Dreiser's own unvoiced declaration of intent as he began his career as an imaginative writer.

By the end of the summer Henry had a plan. He would move to New York, where he and Dreiser would continue to write for the popular magazines, but each would also attempt to write a novel. And so, back in New York in October 1899, Dreiser, as he later recalled, wrote the words "Sister Carrie" at the top of a leaf of the small yellow sheets he used for his writing at that time, and began. Many modern authors setting out to write a first novel have turned to exploitation of some aspect of their own early lives, both because this material is close at hand and because its truthfulness is seemingly authenticated by the writer's first-hand experience. Dreiser, as he began *Sister Carrie*, does not appear to reflect this truism, since the story he was to tell was that of his sister Emma. But by the time Dreiser completed *Sister Carrie*, both Carrie and Hurstwood had become so expressive of his own conception of himself, and especially of his hopes and fears, that their stories had indeed in essence become his own story.

Emma Wilhelmina, the second of Dreiser's five sisters, was eight years older than Theodore. Like all the Dreiser children (Dreiser also had four brothers), at least as Dreiser remembered them, she had resented the restrictions of small town life and of her father's strict religious moralism and had rebelled. Rebellion in her case took the form of leaving home for Chicago, where in early 1886, after some years of living with an architect, she had established a relationship with L. A. Hopkins. Hopkins worked for Chapin and Gore, a firm which owned a number of prominent Chicago saloons; he also had a wife and children. The affair between Emma and Hopkins moved in the direction of domestic farce when Mrs. Hopkins hired a detective to follow her husband. One night, when Hopkins's location had been determined, she and a policeman confronted Emma and Hopkins in bed. ("My God! ma, is that you?" one newspaper report had Hopkins exclaiming.)[2] In response, Hopkins engineered an escape – after taking some $3,500 from his employer's safe, he and Emma (with Emma a willing participant) fled by train for Canada en route to New York. Motivated either by close pursuit or cold feet, Hopkins returned almost all the money while he and Emma were still in Montreal, at which point they were permitted to continue to New York without further police action. By the time Dreiser arrived in New York in late 1894, Hopkins and Emma were in poor circumstances. Hopkins appeared to be permanently out of work, and Emma was unhappily running a seedy rooming house. Several months later Dreiser played a major role in a ruse which permitted Emma to leave Hopkins, who then disappeared from view. Emma herself was later to marry and become a stout working-class housewife.

Dreiser's impulse, in turning to Emma and Hopkins's Chicago

experiences as the basis for the first half of *Sister Carrie*, was not merely to tell a piquant and "true" story but also to use the story to express a more abstract truth – one concerning the nature of life in a great American city in which individuals of varying makeups have their natures clarified and their fates shaped by the raw forces of life. To this end, Dreiser "refined" the characters and experiences of Emma and Hopkins in his portrayal of Carrie and Hurstwood in order to have them serve as more expressive vehicles for his theme. Carrie is made more sensitive and emotional and Hurstwood more socially prominent. In addition, the clear-cut sexual and larcenous nature of the departure of Emma and Hopkins from Chicago is made more complex and ambiguous. Dreiser in these very significant changes was not motivated principally by a desire to remove the gross elements from a true story to make it more palatable to a late Victorian audience. As becomes clear in his depiction of Carrie and Hurstwood's New York experiences, he rather sensed from the beginning in Emma and Hopkins the configuration of inner strength disguised by outer weakness and of outer prominence disguising inner weakness which were the essential truths of their natures, once the "forces of life" present in a large city revealed these truths. For the Chicago portion of the novel, therefore, it was necessary to render Carrie more appealing and Hurstwood more successful than had been true of Emma and Hopkins. And for the New York portion it was necessary to discard entirely the later experiences of Emma and Hopkins because these did not fulfill the expectations about the fates of Carrie and Hurstwood which Dreiser had laid out in the Chicago portion. For the second half of the novel, Dreiser therefore drew upon the deepest strains in his own nature to complete the expression of the themes he saw inherent in his reshaped version of the lives of Emma and Hopkins. Carrie is no longer merely country innocence adrift but an aspiring creative sensibility seeking fulfillment in the artistic marketplace of the metropolis (as was Dreiser); and Hurstwood becomes (as Dreiser had feared he himself might become) a figure broken by the anonymous hostility of the city as he seeks to make his way in a new and more difficult world.

The story of Emma and Hopkins, in short, was transformed by Dreiser into a full-scale fictional exploration of his lifelong preoccupation with the nature of desire, as that aspect of experience is expressed in its varying forms in varying temperaments and as it is shaped in its expression by the distinctive character of American life. In particular, for *Sister Carrie* the late nineteenth-century cultural myths of the seduction of the young girl in the city and of the prosperous origins of the Bowery bum were molded by Dreiser into a complex mix of acceptance and parody of popular belief – one of the principal characteristics of all his fiction from *Sister Carrie* to *An American Tragedy.* For the New York portion of the novel, Dreiser also relied heavily on objective correlatives of desire fulfilled or thwarted that he knew at first hand – the Broadway world of the musical comedy, which he had frequently reported for *Ev'ry Month,* and his own "hard times" trying to break into New York newspaper work during the winter of 1894–95. But in the end, of course, it was Dreiser's identification not only with the externals of the story – with Carrie hunting for a job in Chicago, as Dreiser had done, or with Hurstwood in New York anxiously counting his money, as Dreiser had done – but also with its underlying configuration of hope and fear which is the source of the enduring power of the work.

With Arthur Henry on hand offering encouragement and with Jug reading and correcting portions of the manuscript as Dreiser completed them, *Sister Carrie* went steadily forward. There were of course points at which Dreiser had difficulty – when Hurstwood and Carrie first meet, and when Hurstwood steals the money – and he also had to interrupt his writing to prepare the popular articles that kept the pot boiling. But on the whole he wrote rapidly during the three six-week periods he devoted wholly to the novel and finished a first draft on March 29, 1900. This version of *Sister Carrie* concludes with Hurstwood's suicide and with a strong suggestion in the penultimate chapter that Carrie and Ames are to become romantically involved. In an interview conducted in 1907, Dreiser recalled that he sensed soon after completing this version of the novel that the "book was not done. The narrative, I felt, was finished, but not completed. . . . The story had to stop, and yet I wanted in the final picture to suggest the continuation of Carrie's fate along the lines of established truths."[3] These truths, it was now clear to him – though they had perhaps been suggested initially by Henry and Jug – required that Ames not be considered a "matrimonial possibility"[4] and that the novel end with a summary comment on Carrie. He therefore extensively rewrote the last encounter between Ames and Carrie and expanded an existing brief passage on Carrie beginning "Oh blind strivings of the human heart" into a full-blown epilogue on her nature and fate. Although some recent commentators have favored the abrupt starkness of Dreiser's original ending, and although the sentimental and clichéd diction of Dreiser's apostrophe to Carrie has had few admirers, Dreiser's revision of the conclusion can be defended on several grounds. His removal of an intimation that Carrie and Ames would find happiness together was necessary given his emphasis throughout the novel upon the fact that Carrie's relationships with men eventually become encumbrances hindering her further search for fulfillment. And Dreiser also appears to have felt strongly that his role as prophet,[5] as interpreter of the larger significance of the life he had portrayed, required him, as a kind of aesthetic necessity to the overall tone and shape of the novel, to offer a last reading of Carrie's essential character and destiny. Indeed, he was to conclude all his major novels with a similar kind of epilogue.

Even before Dreiser finished the first draft of *Sister Carrie*, the novel was being typed. What happened after the typescript was completed in mid or late April 1900 is at the center of a major difference of opinion among Dreiser scholars. In all of Dreiser's own accounts – including his specific recollection of the chronology to his first biographer Dorothy Dudley[6] – he and Henry realized, once the book was fully typed, that it was too long. (In its later cut form, *Sister Carrie* was a book of 557 pages in the Doubleday, Page first edition. In its uncut typescript form, it was approximately 36,000 words longer, or about 680 printed pages, which would have made it exceptionally long by the standards of the day, especially for a first novel by an unknown author.) This desire to shorten the novel also introduced the possibility of improving it. Like most novice writers of fiction, Dreiser had overextended a number of incidents and authorial explanations early in the novel in an effort to establish fully his characters and their situation. In addition, he now realized that some Chicago incidents and passages which derived from Emma and Hopkins's lives and which therefore suggested a coarse element in Hurstwood and Carrie's experiences were inappropriate in light of his later depiction of Hurstwood's tragic fall and Carrie's growth in sensibility. These various motives led Dreiser and Henry to concentrate on shortening the Chicago portion of the novel. Henry played an initial and important role in this effort by reading through the typescript and suggesting passages for omission. Dreiser then accepted or rejected these suggestions. After the novel was cut, it was submitted for publication to Harper and Brothers, which rejected it.

A different interpretation both of the chronology and of the motives behind the cutting of *Sister Carrie* is offered by the editors of the recent Pennsylvania Edition. In this account of the prepublication history of the novel, Dreiser submitted *Sister Carrie* to Harper and Brothers *before* he and Henry cut the novel.[7] When Harpers rejected the book because Dreiser had not been sufficiently "delicate" in depicting the "illicit relations of the heroine" and because the novel would not hold the interest of "the feminine readers who control the destiny of so many novels,"[8] Dreiser was persuaded by Henry to revise *Sister Carrie* to make it more consistent with popular taste. Thus, the editors of the Pennsylvania Edition argue, Dreiser in effect served as his own censor to the extent that his cutting weakened the sexual honesty and philosophical depth of the novel. In response to this interpretation, the Pennsylvania Edition prints as the authoritative text of *Sister Carrie* the holograph manuscript before Dreiser revised its ending and before he and Henry cut the novel.

This is a plausible and appealing argument, but as this author and several other reviewers of the Pennsylvania Edition have noted, it has several major flaws.[9] First, there is no external evidence to support a belief that *Sister Carrie* was cut in response to its rejection by Harpers. Second, if it was Dreiser and Henry's intent to make the novel more acceptable to a feminine audience, they failed miserably. It was after all Mrs. Doubleday, in a legend which probably has an element of truth to it, who demanded that her husband seek to suppress the novel despite his firm's acceptance of it. And a repeated note in reviews of the 1900 edition was that the novel was "unpleasant" – a code term intended to put the delicate prospective reader on her guard. Third, is it possible to reject an author's own revisions on the grounds that he made them poorly? It is the author's book in the end, and except when there is clear evidence of coercion – as there is not in this instance – his motives for revision must be treated with the same respect as those which led him to write the book in the first place. Otherwise, common sense tells us, we as editors will be attempting to substitute our own critical judgment for the author's creative imagination, which expresses itself as much in revision as in original composition. And finally, it has not been demonstrated that the Pennsylvania Edition of *Sister Carrie* is a better book than the Doubleday, Page version. It is longer and more detailed and more explicit, but these qualities, as commentators have also pointed out, do not necessarily make a better novel.

Harpers, in its letter of rejection, had commented somewhat disparagingly on the "realism" of *Sister Carrie*. It was perhaps with this characterization in mind that Dreiser then submitted the novel to Doubleday, Page and Company, a new firm that had been formed earlier in 1900 after the dissolution of Doubleday and McClure. In that reorganization, Frank Norris, whose novel *McTeague* had been published by Doubleday and McClure in 1899, went with Frank Doubleday and was serving as a part-time manuscript reader while still pursuing a career as a novelist. *McTeague,* much of which depicts the decline of a San Francisco dentist and his wife into poverty, violence, and sexual degradation, was "realism" with a vengeance. Norris was assigned to read *Sister Carrie,* and he liked it very much. He wrote Dreiser in late May that "the book pleased me as well as any novel I have ever read" and that he would enthusiastically recommend its publication.[10] Doubleday himself was out of the country, and in his absence Walter H. Page, the firm's junior partner, met with Dreiser in early June and informed him of the novel's acceptance. Elated, Dreiser left for Missouri with his wife to visit her family, and he and Henry quickly spread the news that Doubleday, Page was to publish the novel.

It is at this point that the story of the publication of *Sister Carrie* becomes part of twentieth-century American cultural mythology. As Dreiser later recounted the tale again and again,[11] Doubleday, on his return from Europe in mid-July, took the typescript of the novel home to read. There, Mrs. Doubleday, a woman active in social work, read it and found it offensive. Doubleday agreed with her and informed Page that the firm should not publish *Sister Carrie* because, as Norris told Henry, he "thinks the story is immoral and badly written."[12] Because Page had accepted the novel, however, it was necessary to persuade Dreiser to withdraw it, and this Page attempted to do, during late July and early August, in several conversations with Henry and in a number of lengthy letters to Dreiser. But Dreiser remained adamant that he wished the firm to honor its word, and so at last, on August 20, after Dreiser's return from Missouri, a contract was signed. This, however, did not end Dreiser's difficulties with Doubleday, Page. The firm had asked from the start that Dreiser change many of the names of actual places and people mentioned in the novel, and it now pressed this demand even more insistently. Dreiser resisted this effort, and thus, in a still-obscure series of revisions and re-revisions of the typescript and the missing proof, some names were changed and some were not. In addition, as Dreiser claimed to have learned at a later date from the firm's lawyer, Doubleday had been advised that the firm's legal obligations under the contract ended with publication. He was not required to push the novel through advertising or any other means, and he did not. As a result, only 456 copies of *Sister Carrie* were sold in the first sixteen months after its publication, producing a total royalty of $68.40.

It has never been possible to authenticate the role of Mrs. Doubleday in the "suppression" of *Sister Carrie*. Her name does not appear in any of the extensive correspondence about the novel during the summer of 1900, and Doubleday himself later denied to Franklin Walker, the biographer of Frank Norris, that there was any truth to the story of her involvement. But Dreiser believed it, and he told it to so many interviewers and correspondents during the course of his career (he also published several versions of the story during the 1920s and 1930s)[13] that its authenticity was widely accepted. (As early as 1907, a review of the second edition of *Sister Carrie* could be headlined, "Triumphant Vindication of a Suppressed Novel.") In this legendary account of the battle between Art and Philistinism, Dreiser and Norris (Dreiser later omitted Henry's important role)[14] fight a rearguard battle for Truth against Mrs. Doubleday, who stands for all that is oppressive in

American middle-class moralism. Thus, though the myth of the suppression of *Sister Carrie* may not be literally true (Mrs. Doubleday's role is obscure, and Doubleday did in fact publish the book), the myth contains a truth of its own, that of the belief by most early twentieth-century American artists in the permanent struggle — earlier often lost, now increasingly victorious — for artistic freedom in America.

Sister Carrie was published by Doubleday, Page on November 8, 1900. The firm's records reveal that over 100 copies were sent out for review (it was probably Norris who made certain that review copies were distributed), and in fact the standard Dreiser bibliography records twenty-six reviews in American magazines and newspapers between publication and March 1901. A good many of these were brief paragraphs, and others were devoted principally to retelling the plot of the novel, but enough substantial reviews appeared to indicate a number of common responses to *Sister Carrie*.[15] Many of the reviewers found the novel "gloomy" or "unhealthful," and, as noted earlier, "unpleasant" also occurs frequently, usually referring to Dreiser's uncritical depiction of Carrie's illicit relationships. Nevertheless, a surprisingly large number of reviewers were startled into appreciative responses, some of which still constitute basic issues in the criticism of the novel. "Told with an unsparing realism and detail," the reviewer of the Newark *Sunday News* remarked, "it has all the interest of fact; and the terrible inevitableness of fact also. . . . The impression is simply one of truth, and therein lies at once the strength and horror of it."[16] In addition, as has been true for the entire critical history of *Sister Carrie*, most reviewers found the portrait of Carrie problematical in meaning and effect, while Hurstwood's decline was almost universally praised for its grim truth. The excessive length of the novel was often remarked upon, and Dreiser's "annoying anachronisms and blunders in English"[17] were frequently cited, with several reviewers providing extensive examples.

Dreiser was sensitive to criticism and often replied to it, as he did to two of the most frequent negative comments on *Sister Carrie* by its reviewers. To a St. Louis newspaper interviewer who remarked in January 1902 that *Sister Carrie* had been attacked "upon the score of morality," Dreiser replied: "In 'Sister Carrie' all the phases of life touched upon are handled truthfully. I have not tried to gloss over any evil any more than I have stopped to dwell upon it."[18] He told another interviewer in June 1907, on the publication of the second edition of *Sister Carrie:*

> Here is a book that is close to life. It is intended not as a piece of literary craftsmanship, but as a picture of conditions done as simply and effectively as the English language will permit. To set up and criticize me for saying "vest" instead of waistcoat, to talk about my splitting the infinitive and using vulgar commonplaces here and there, when the tragedy of a man's life is being depicted, is silly.[19]

Sister Carrie was published in London by William Heinemann in late July 1901 as part of Heinemann's Dollar Library series. Heinemann was much interested in American writers (he had helped launch Stephen Crane's career by the publication of the English edition of *The Red Badge of Courage* in 1895), and his Dollar Library series was devoted to new American authors. Because books in the series were uniformly and cheaply priced, Dreiser was asked to shorten the novel. This task again fell on Henry, and in this instance Dreiser played no role in the cutting. Although *Sister Carrie* was not widely reviewed in England, it did receive very favorable reviews from several major journals, including the *Academy, Athenaeum,* and *Spectator,* with a number of reviewers noting that it was the best work to appear in the Dollar Library. By September, the New York *Commercial Advertiser* could comment on the critical success of the novel in England.

Despite his difficulties with Doubleday, Page, Dreiser now considered himself principally a novelist. Even before the American publication of *Sister Carrie,* he had begun to plan his second novel, the work that was to become *Jennie Gerhardt.* But he also realized that if *Sister Carrie* was to play a role in establishing him as a novelist, he would have to gain control of the book from Doubleday, Page. In the spring of 1901 Dreiser therefore signed a contract with the firm of J. F. Taylor and Company not only for the publication of *Jennie Gerhardt* but for the reissuing of *Sister Carrie,* and to this end Taylor purchased the stereotype plates of the novel from Doubleday, Page. Taylor's plan of first publishing *Jennie Gerhardt* and then reissuing *Sister Carrie* never came to fruition, however; Dreiser suffered some form of nervous breakdown in the summer of 1901

13

and was unable to complete *Jennie Gerhardt*. After several difficult years, Dreiser got back on his feet and by 1907 was a successful magazine editor. He now returned to his plan to republish *Sister Carrie*, and the novel was at last reissued in 1907 by B. W. Dodge, a firm in which Dreiser had an interest. *Sister Carrie* has remained in print ever since. It was republished in the Modern Library series in 1932, and it appeared as a Limited Editions Club volume in 1939, with illustrations by Reginald Marsh. The first modern paperback edition of the novel was published by Pocket Books in 1949. More than twenty translations of *Sister Carrie* have been published, and the novel is presently available in English in over a dozen different editions.

Dreiser's work, and especially *Sister Carrie*, has been central to discussions of the nature of twentieth-century American life since his reputation as a leading American writer became established about the time of the First World War. Dreiser had returned to fiction in 1911 with *Jennie Gerhardt*, and after the publication of the first two novels of the Cowperwood trilogy, *The Financier* (1912) and *The Titan* (1914), and especially after the furor caused by the supposed licentiousness of *The "Genius"* (1915), Dreiser's work, ideas, and public stances have figured prominently in various bitter disputes occurring at "the dark and bloody crossroads," as Lionel Trilling put it, "where literature and politics meet."[20] Or, stated somewhat differently, Dreiser's capacity for expressing provocative major ideas about man and society, as well as the issues for literary criticism raised by his fictional method, have made his works touchstones both of belief and of literary form at several major moments in twentieth-century American cultural history.

The first such moment occurred during the late teens and early 1920s, when Dreiser's willingness to explore the full range of American life, as exemplified by Hurstwood's decline to a Bowery bum and Carrie's illicit affairs, served as the basis for an angry debate on the relationship between literature and public morality. One group of writers, led by H. L. Mencken and including Sinclair Lewis and Randolph Bourne, championed Dreiser as the figure who would help to batter down the last vestiges of Puritan moralism in America. "The feet of Dreiser are making a path for us," Sherwood Anderson wrote in 1916. "They are tramping through the wilderness making a path."[21] To others, however, Dreiser was less a pathfinder than an agent of regression in his dramatization of the triumph of man's "animal" nature over his capacity for reason and moral choice. Stuart P. Sherman made the case for condemnation of Dreiser on these grounds in his famous essay of 1915, "The Naturalism of Mr. Dreiser" (an essay which Sherman later more polemically titled "The Barbaric Naturalism of Theodore Dreiser"), in which he charged that Dreiser had eliminated "distinctively human values" and had made "animal instincts the supreme factor in human life."[22] During the early 1920s Sherman's use of Dreiser to attack much modern fiction (as well as much modern life) as morally suspect was frequently endorsed by a group of academic critics, led by Paul Elmer More and Irving Babbitt, who came to be known as the New Humanists.

Events, however, overtook this debate. It became fatuous to call for a literature which stressed man's capacity for rational moral choice when an entire generation of great novelists, including James Joyce, Thomas Mann, Marcel Proust, and the early William Faulkner, were demonstrating the tragic power of the irrational in human affairs. By the early 1930s, the use of Dreiser's work to argue major issues in American life had shifted from the ethical to the political and literary. Like most writers of the time, Dreiser in the late 1920s had become absorbed in social and political matters and had adopted many of the ideas and causes of the far left; during the 1930s he was often regarded as the principal American literary spokesman of the left. But unlike most American writers, who, as the decade came to a close with such dispiriting events as the Moscow treason trials and the Nazi-Russian pact, to say nothing of the domination of the American Communist Party by rigid Stalinist loyalists, began to leave the movement, Dreiser remained and became an increasingly isolated figure of unswerving commitment to the party line. Indeed, in a widely reported symbolic act, the aged and ailing Dreiser officially joined the Communist party in July 1945, some five months before his death.

The stage was thus set for another dismissal of Dreiser and his work because of his inherent limitations of mind – now his limitations of intellect rather than of moral insight. Writers who, like Dreiser, had been attracted by the radical left but who, unlike Dreiser, had then repudiated this affiliation, saw in his failure to recognize the flaws of communism a deeper failure of perception into the nature of things. Some of them also no doubt found in Dreiser a convenient scapegoat, helping to cleanse their own earlier lapses in political wisdom. The principal document in this widespread attack on Dreiser during the late 1940s and 1950s was Lionel Trilling's "Reality in America," an essay which is perhaps the most generally known discussion of Dreiser ever published.[23] Trilling was deeply troubled that Dreiser, as evidenced by his obituaries and by the cordial reception afforded his posthumous novel *The Bulwark,* still had some standing among liberal critics. He was also disturbed by his awareness that F. O. Matthiessen, one of the most distinguished academic critics of the day, was preparing a full-length appreciative study of Dreiser. It was therefore necessary, Trilling believed, to reveal that the emperor had no clothes. Dreiser had always been praised for his recognition of the material basis of experience, but this praise, Trilling argued, ignored the vulgarity and emptiness of Dreiser's ideas because some of these ideas coincided with those of the radical left. Dreiser's fiction, in short, was analogous to communism in its simplistic view of life, a view which failed to take cognizance of the role of the mental or spiritual in human affairs.

It is now clear – and indeed it was clear as early as 1955, when Alfred Kazin commented perceptively on Trilling's essay[24] – that Trilling's attack derived principally from his contempt for the mindless political orthodoxy that he found both in Dreiser's beliefs during the 1930s and in the critical estimates of his work by left-leaning critics during that decade, an orthodoxy that does not in fact inform Dreiser's major novels. Nevertheless, Trilling's assault on Dreiser's beliefs, combined with the seeming incompatibility of Dreiser's fictional methods with the critical interests of the then-dominant New Criticism, brought Dreiser's reputation during the 1940s and 1950s to its lowest state. Both Trilling and the New Criticism demanded that literature render the complexities of life in a complex manner (Henry James and T. S. Eliot reached the height of their reputations during this period), and Dreiser was held to be deficient in this quality. As Irving Howe later recalled, during the 1940s and 1950s Dreiser's work was "a symbol of everything a superior intelligence was supposed to avoid."[25]

In fact, however, academic criticism and scholarship were not completely avoiding Dreiser even during the 1950s, and by the late 1960s he had become the subject of a number of significant studies. The intent of much of this criticism was to rescue Dreiser's fiction from a superficial association with the moral, philosophical, and political stances Dreiser expressed elsewhere and thus to reveal that the "power" which most readers had always found in his novels indeed resided in his fictional themes and techniques. To fulfill this goal, it was initially necessary to refine the conception of literary naturalism – naturalism both as an American literary movement and as the distinctive element in Dreiser's fiction – since almost from the beginning of his career various simplistic definitions of naturalism had been used as a club to bludgeon Dreiser. As early as 1938, Eliseo Vivas, in a ground-breaking essay, located Dreiser's "inconsistent mechanism" as the source of his fictional strength;[26] and over the next several decades a number of other critics helped to define the body of ideas in Dreiser's fiction – whether identified as transcendental or romantic – that served to balance his evolutionary and mechanistic beliefs.[27] Another phase in this effort to come to grips with Dreiser's fiction itself rather than to depend on conventional ideas about it was the attempt to discover what in fact constituted his fictional technique. What does it signify that a powerful author writes so badly, Saul Bellow asked in relation to Dreiser in 1951.[28] It signifies, later criticism replied, in various efforts to describe Dreiser's fictional style, that a powerful writer does not write badly. Dreiser may, more than most writers, construct a clumsy sentence now and then, and he had a weakness, especially early in his career (as in the epilogue to *Sister Carrie*) for clichéd sentiment, but he was also capable of a subtle craftsmanship. In *Sister Carrie,* for example, William L. Phillips established a coherent body of imagery guiding our involvement with Carrie,[29] and Julian Markels described Dreiser's ability to introduce an underlying thematic rhythm through the juxtaposition of scenes.[30] Raising the stakes even further, Ellen Moers, in a landmark essay, analyzed the "finesse" of Dreiser in various key

17

scenes in *Sister Carrie*,[31] and Robert Penn Warren extolled the "beautiful precision" of Dreiser's prose style at its best.[32] In a culmination of these efforts, two of the major books on Dreiser published during the 1970s – Warren's *Homage to Theodore Dreiser* (1971) and Donald Pizer's *The Novels of Theodore Dreiser* (1976) – did not find it necessary (as criticism so often had in the past) to apologize for Dreiser's limitations as a novelist or to offer vague notion of his "power" as a compensation for these limitations. The critical emphasis was now on the richness of the novels themselves rather than on their stylistic ineptness or on the presence within them of a crude and monolithic determinism.

During the 1980s, a considerable body of criticism of Dreiser and especially of *Sister Carrie* has concentrated on his work as a reflection of the beliefs and values of his time. Much of this criticism is related to the theoretical position that the writer absorbs from his moment many of its underlying assumptions about class, gender, and social value and that these are then expressed not only in the themes of the work but also in its techniques and language.[33] In a not uncommon turn of fortune's critical wheel, the same Dreiser who was dismissed by a previous generation of critics as too obviously and crudely Marxist in his representation of the individual's subservience to social forces is now the object of studies which reveal the depth and significance of his characters' responsiveness to contemporary social values. Unfortunately, like the earlier Marxist criticism, a good deal of this recent study of Dreiser is still jargon-ridden and thesis-bound. Carrie is often depicted as a dupe of "consumerism" and "commodification," and her lust for objects is proclaimed as the principal theme of the novel.

One of the most characteristic of these recent readings of *Sister Carrie* is Walter Benn Michaels's essay "*Sister Carrie*'s Popular Economy" in his work *The Gold Standard and the Logic of Naturalism* (1987). Michaels, in his central premise that Dreiser unconsciously endorses Carrie's early definition of happiness and success in material terms, returns Dreiser criticism to its former character of a means to attack certain strains in American life. Just as Stuart Sherman, in 1915, stressed Dreiser's "animalism" and ignored his belief in "spirit" in order to attack what Sherman felt was the moral decline of American life, so Michaels and a number of similarly minded recent critics stress Carrie's acquisitiveness and ignore her developing sensibility in order to contend that even Dreiser, a presumed critic of his times, could be swayed by the destructive materialism at the center of American capitalist society. This form of criticism has often contributed to an understanding of *Sister Carrie* despite its obvious limitations, however, since the close study of Carrie and Hurstwood's relationship to their worlds has revealed as seldom before the texture and depth of Dreiser's rendering of the contemporary social context of their lives. And it has also demonstrated once again that *Sister Carrie*, in its archetypal pattern of Carrie's rise and Hurstwood's fall within the life of two great American cities, continues to attract criticism which seeks to discover in the novel those characteristics that reveal the emerging nature of twentieth-century American experience.

The four original essays collected in this volume not only touch upon long-established approaches to *Sister Carrie* but also reflect a number of the concerns of recent scholarship and criticism. It is not surprising that Carrie herself continues to be the focus of much criticism, given her problematic character and her suggestive relationship both to Dreiser's beliefs and to the values of his time. Thus, Thomas P. Riggio explores the sources of Carrie's "blues" in Dreiser's own family and experience in order to demonstrate the depth of Dreiser's psychological portrait, and Barbara Hochman finds in Carrie's career as an actress a key both to her character and to Dreiser's identification with her. Like many recent critics of *Sister Carrie*, both of these writers are engaged by the novel's metaphor of life and art as a form of theater, finding in the complex suggestiveness of the metaphor a rich vein of inquiry. Richard Lehan also devotes much attention to Carrie, but he is more fully occupied by the relationship of Dreiser's fundamental beliefs to the naturalistic form of *Sister Carrie* and by the bearing of this form upon recent criticism which deals both with textual issues and with the historical relevance of the novel. In his concern for the connection between Dreiser's naturalism and the novel's urban setting, Lehan also reveals the seemingly permanent centrality of these two areas of interest in discussions of *Sister Carrie*. Finally, Alan Trachtenberg explores, in an essay which connects the often-discussed issue of Dreiser's narrative style to the more recent interest in his historicism, the ways in which Dreiser as narrative voice deeply involves us in the complex yoking of social information and individual consciousness in the novel.

NOTES

1. The standard biographies of Dreiser are Robert H. Elias, *Theodore Dreiser: Apostle of Nature* (rev. ed., Ithaca, N. Y.: Cornell University Press, 1970); W. A. Swanberg, *Dreiser* (New York: Scribners, 1965); and Richard Lingeman, *Theodore Dreiser: At the Gates of the City, 1871–1907* (New York: Putnam's, 1986) and *Theodore Dreiser: An American Journey, 1908–1945* (New York: Putnam's, 1990). The fullest accounts of the genesis and composition of *Sister Carrie* are contained in Ellen Moers, *Two Dreisers* (New York: Viking, 1969), pp. 3–169; Donald Pizer, *The Novels of Theodore Dreiser: A Critical Study* (Minneapolis: University of Minnesota Press, 1976), pp. 31–51; and James L. W. West III, "*Sister Carrie:* Manuscript to Print," in the Pennsylvania Edition of *Sister Carrie* (Philadelphia: University of Pennsylvania Press, 1981), pp. 503–41.
2. Chicago *Mail*, February 17, 1886, p. 1; reprinted in *Sister Carrie: An Authoritative Text, Background and Sources, Criticism*, ed. Donald Pizer (New York: Norton, 1970), p. 376. This edition reprints a number of newspaper accounts of the theft.
3. New York *Herald*, July 7, 1907, p. 2; reprinted in *Sister Carrie*, ed. Pizer, p. 432.
4. The phrase is found among the notes which Dreiser used to revise the conclusion of *Sister Carrie;* see West, Pennsylvania Edition, p. 516.
5. The quasi-philosophical observations which Dreiser wrote for each issue of *Ev'ry Month* were entitled "Reflections" and signed "The Prophet."
6. Dorothy Dudley, *Dreiser and the Land of the Free* (New York: Beechhurst Press, 1946), p. 162. Dudley dated the conversation July 1930.
7. West, Pennsylvania Edition, pp. 519–22.
8. West, Pennsylvania Edition, p. 519.
9. See, in particular, reviews by Donald Pizer, *American Literature* 53 (January 1982): 731–77; Stephen Brennan, *Studies in the Novel* 14 (Summer 1982): 211–13; and Richard Brodhead, *Yale Review* 71 (Summer 1982): 597–600. Donald Pizer also discusses at length Dreiser's supposed self-censorship of *Sister Carrie* in his "Self-Censorship and Textual Editing," in *Textual Criticism and Literary Interpretation*, ed.

Jerome J. McGann (Chicago: University of Chicago Press, 1985), pp. 144–61.

10. *Sister Carrie*, ed. Pizer, p. 434. This edition also reprints the correspondence among Dreiser, Henry, Page, and Doubleday referred to in the following paragraphs.

11. The first account of the legend by Dreiser which I have found occurs in a January 1902 interview, "Author of *Sister Carrie*," St. Louis *Post-Dispatch*, January 26, 1902, p. 4; reprinted in *Sister Carrie*, ed. Pizer, p. 456.

12. Henry to Dreiser, July 19, 1900; in *Sister Carrie*, ed. Pizer, p. 437.

13. Perhaps the most commonly known version is "The Early Adventures of *Sister Carrie*," Dreiser's introduction to the 1932 Modern Library edition of *Sister Carrie;* the introduction is reprinted in *Sister Carrie*, ed. Pizer, pp. 463–5.

14. Dreiser had broken with Henry in 1902, in part because of Henry's unflattering portrait of Dreiser in Henry's novel *An Island Cabin* (1902). Dreiser thereafter seldom mentioned Henry; he also removed from later editions of *Sister Carrie* the dedication to Henry which appeared in the Doubleday, Page first edition.

15. A large sampling of these reviews is reprinted in *Theodore Dreiser: The Critical Reception*, ed. Jack Salzman (New York: David Lewis, 1972).

16. Newark *Sunday News*, September 1, 1901, magazine section, p. 2; reprinted in *Theodore Dreiser*, ed. Salzman, pp. 15–16.

17. Chicago *Daily Tribune*, February 25, 1901, p. 6; reprinted in *Theodore Dreiser*, ed. Salzman, p. 14.

18. "Author of *Sister Carrie*," St. Louis *Post-Dispatch*, January 26, 1902, p. 4; reprinted in *Sister Carrie*, ed. Pizer, p. 458.

19. Otis Notman, "Talks with Four Novelists: Mr. Dreiser," *New York Times Saturday Review of Books*, January 15, 1907, p. 393; reprinted in *Theodore Dreiser: A Selection of Uncollected Prose*, ed. Donald Pizer (Detroit: Wayne State University Press, 1977), p. 174.

20. Trilling, "Reality in America," *The Liberal Imagination* (New York: Viking, 1950); reprinted in *Critical Essays on Theodore Dreiser*, ed. Donald Pizer (Boston: G. K. Hall, 1981), p. 38.

21. Anderson, "Dreiser," *Little Review* 3 (April 1916): 5; reprinted in *Critical Essays*, ed. Pizer, p. 13.

22. Sherman, "The Naturalism of Mr. Dreiser," *Nation* 101 (December 2, 1915): 648–50; reprinted in *Critical Essays*, ed. Pizer, p. 9.

23. The Dreiser portion of Trilling's essay, an essay which also included an attack on V. L. Parrington, was published initially in *The Nation* in

1946. The entire essay appeared for the first time in Trilling's widely read *The Liberal Imagination* (New York: Viking, 1950).

24. See Kazin's introduction to *The Stature of Theodore Dreiser,* ed. Alfred Kazin and Charles Shapiro (Bloomington: Indiana University Press, 1955), p. 10; reprinted in *Critical Essays,* ed. Pizer, p. 53.

25. Howe, "An American Tragedy," *The New Republic* 151 (July 26, 1964): 19; reprinted in *Critical Essays,* ed. Pizer, p. 292.

26. Vivas, "Dreiser, An Inconsistent Mechanist," *Ethics* 48 (July 1938): 498–508; reprinted in *Critical Essays,* ed. Pizer, pp. 30–37.

27. See in particular Charles C. Walcutt, *American Literary Naturalism, A Divided Stream* (Minneapolis: University of Minnesota Press, 1956); Donald Pizer, *Realism and Naturalism in Nineteenth-Century American Literature* (Carbondale: Southern Illinois University Press, 1966; rev. ed., 1984); and Richard Lehan, *Theodore Dreiser: His World and His Novels* (Carbondale: Southern Illinois University Press, 1969).

28. Bellow, "Dreiser and the Triumph of Art," *Commentary* 11 (May 1951): 50; reprinted in *Stature,* ed. Kazin and Shapiro, p. 146.

29. Phillips, "The Imagery of Dreiser's Novels," *PMLA* 78 (December 1963): 572–85.

30. Markels, "Dreiser and the Plotting of Inarticulate Experience," *Massachusetts Review* 2 (Spring 1961): 431–48.

31. Moers, "The Finesse of Dreiser," *American Scholar* 33 (Winter 1963): 109–14.

32. Warren, *Homage to Theodore Dreiser* (New York: Random House, 1971), p. 27.

33. Among studies of this kind are Rachel Bowlby, *Just Looking: Consumer Culture in Dreiser, Gissing, and Zola* (New York: Methuen, 1985); Robert Shulman, *Social Criticism in Nineteenth-Century American Fictions* (Columbia: University of Missouri Press, 1987); and Amy Kaplan, *The Social Construction of American Realism* (Chicago: University of Chicago Press, 1988).

2

Carrie's Blues

THOMAS P. RIGGIO

. . . the curious effect which Carrie's blues had upon the part.
                                                    —*Sister Carrie*

1

WHAT most struck *Sister Carrie*'s first readers was the clarity and understanding that Dreiser brought to the figure of Hurstwood. The novel's heroine, however, puzzled many reviewers, who found her to be, as William Marion Reedy put it, "real" but "paradoxically . . . shadowy."[1] Words like "shadowy," "nebulous," "paradoxical" expressed the uneasiness early critics felt about the character. Even the book's admirers tended to think that its "extraordinary power . . . has little to do with the delineation of foolish, worldly wise Carrie."[2] There was, moreover, little agreement about what sort of woman Carrie represented: some saw her as "calloused" and driven by "hard cold selfishness," while others used terms of endearment that matched Dreiser's own sentimental language for his "waif amid forces."[3] Ninety years later, the situation hasn't changed much. The contradictions in Carrie's character — a narcissistic young woman in whom self-interest runs high, yet who on "her spiritual side . . . was rich in feeling . . . for the weak and the helpless"[4] — have encouraged critics to see her as everything from a Victorian vamp and golddigger to "a naive, dreaming girl from the country, driven this way and that by the promptings of biology and economy, and pursued on her course by the passions of her rival lovers."[5]

Some readers attribute the wide range of critical responses to what they consider the young author's shaky grasp of Carrie's makeup. Behind this judgment lies a more general sense that Dreiser possesses as F. O. Matthiessen said, "very little of the psychologist's skill in portraying the inner life of his characters."[6] Certainly

Dreiser's way of assigning motivation to characters lends itself to this charge. In the post-Freudian literary culture that shaped our views of the novelist, Dreiser's insistence on the physiological determinants of mental states and his habit of building narrative around characters' responses to environmental stimuli have led to assumptions of psychological naiveté.

Figures like Hurstwood and Clyde Griffith tend to be treated as exceptions to Matthiessen's point, mainly because Dreiser is most skillful at character analysis when he can unite his naturalistic themes to stories of psychic and social dissolution. Hurstwood's psychology, for example, unfolds under conditions so absolute that they do indeed seem to determine his fate: mid-life crisis, the effects of an emotionally arid family life, the lure of a young woman, the influence of alcohol, the stress of isolation, and the depression that follows upon business ruin and the loss of social identity. Placed in an industrial urban America that had not yet developed the rudiments of modern social services, Hurstwood's movement to skid row and suicide is historically appropriate as well. And yet, despite the sense of inevitability that accompanies these external forces, Dreiser's overriding sense that character is destiny remains the central fact of Hurstwood's story. Put another way, Dreiser never allows us to forget that the major determinant of Hurstwood's tragedy, what gives his case its compelling logic, is that his was a mind "not trained to reason or introspect" or to "analyze the change that was taking place in his mind and hence his body" (339).

With Carrie Meeber, Dreiser set out to write a different and subtler story, one that demanded a more complex psychology than his physiological analysis could account for. Dreiser's problem was to draw a character for whom the regressive self-seeking need for the commodities and comforts that constitute the "good life" in America is increasingly in tension with the positive, though often misguided, quest for "beauty" and self-expression. The contradictions in Carrie that disturb many critics were for Dreiser the central drama of her inner life. She is a character whose destiny is unclear because her identity, from beginning to end, is only in the process of being formed.

Carrie's identity may be in perpetual flux, but she possesses one trait that, like a Renaissance character caught in the grip of a prevailing humour, essentially defines her. Near the end of the novel, Robert Ames, who comes closest to being Dreiser's voice in the novel, submits to Carrie "one of those keen observations which was the result of his comprehension of her nature." He recommends Hardy's novels to her, because she shares with them a "gloomy" mood. But he quickly corrects himself: "'Not exactly gloomy,' he added. 'There's another word – melancholia, sad. I should judge you were rather lonely in your disposition'" (481). At the end Carrie remains melancholy, as she begins to see that all she has aspired to, including fame, cannot satisfy her needs. As she leaves Ames, who is showing a good deal of interest in her, she feels not hope or elation but "very much alone, very much as if she were struggling hopelessly and unaided, as if such a man as he would never care to draw nearer. . . . She was already the old, mournful Carrie – the desireful Carrie, – unsatisfied" (487).

The old, mournful Carrie. Ames's "keen observation" describes Carrie's essential character, not just an effect of her time in the city. Ignoring the psychological aspects of her character, criticism has traditionally centered on the economic and social facets of Carrie's rise with its classic contrast in the decline of Hurstwood.[7] But a stress upon the importance of the despairing, melancholic side of Carrie's mind, in which the emphasis is on an inner "fall" that coexists with the famous rise, suggests the extent to which in Dreiser's fiction the exterior sources of misery (and pleasure) are finally at the mercy of more potent inner conflicts. What distinguished Dreiser in 1900 from his more socially progressive contemporaries like Upton Sinclair and Jack London is that in his writing such factors as poverty, class conflict, the plight of women and workers – all the forces that drive Carrie – are not so much condemned as they are accepted, and even welcomed, as occasions to dramatize preexisting states of mind.

To say this is to recognize Dreiser as a psychological realist, as much attuned to the psychic tensions within his characters as to the powerful social and physical agents that attend their careers. This is not to deny what everyone recognizes as Dreiser's tenacious attachment to a tangible world teeming with such forces, or the powerful hold this world exerts on his characters. Carrie is often shown as a victim of external events, and particularly in her responses to men she appears to be dominated "by conditions over which [she] had little control" (106). These conditions take on the power of universal law, to the extent that Dreiser often pays for his reliance on such forces with a certain lack of individualization, and at times just fuzzy thought. The novel's plot hinges on factors like the turn of the seasons, so that in *Sister Carrie* it is axiomatic that the "fall" always follows winter. The story is crowded with such contingencies, which keep Carrie so busy fighting off deprivations at the Hansons – joblessness, illness, abduction, poverty – that she has little time for self-scrutiny. Carrie's obsessive worries about clothes, money, and shelter keep in the foreground the city's hypnotic effect on her and displace from the center of her consciousness any extended reflection on the origin of her pains.

Yet these forces function effectively in the novel precisely because psychologically they suggest the original sources of Carrie's melancholy. Winter approaches, but even in the security of her new flat Carrie feels old fears that beset her alone: "Somehow the swaying of some dead branches of trees across the way brought back the picture she was familiar with, when she looked from their front window in December days at home. She paused and wrung her little hands" (76). The city, in all its social density, offers a host of such unsettling forces, which Dreiser in his best books (including those about himself) uses to explore the ways his already maimed, anxious dreamers meet their fates.

A problem develops, however, when we try to locate the origins of Carrie's conflicted nature.[8] The difficulty arises in part because Dreiser deliberately obscures the details of Carrie's life in Wisconsin – a strange omission for a writer who stressed the importance of formative years on the development of character. All we *see* of her Columbia City relations is contained in part of one sentence: "A gush of tears at her mother's farewell kiss, a touch in her throat when the cars clacked by the flour mill where her father worked by the day, a pathetic sigh as the familiar green environs of the village passed in review" (3). These verbal snapshots of family and hometown leave us with unanswered questions about their relation to Carrie's later career. What these people and places have to do with Carrie's decision to leave; how her compulsive desire for clothes and material goods might reflect certain deprivations as a child; why she might be attracted to men who provide such things; why she is depressed or feels worthless without them; why winter oppresses her; why she attempts unsuccessfully to reestablish herself as part of a family, first with Minnie, then in "marriage" to Drouet and later to Hurstwood; why she keeps Ames at a distance; or what the experience of separation may have had to do with all this – Dreiser rarely makes such questions part of Carrie's conscious thought.

Carrie's lack of reflection on such matters has led Ellen Moers – who otherwise thought that the "central fact about Dreiser's work" is that he "wrote like a brother"[9] – to conclude that Carrie's story was strangely not about "daughter and parents," that such relations are "notably absent not only from the foreground of the novel but also from the background of his heroine's mind."[10] The note of surprise is warranted. We know from his writing about other sisters, brothers, and parents that for Dreiser the ties to home were never light or easily broken. My argument is that Dreiser not only wrote like a brother in the creation of his first fictional sister; but also, with a good deal of psychological insight, he built his heroine's inner life around family relations that are very much in the background of her mind.

2

The first chapter of *Sister Carrie* gives us a glimpse of Carrie at the moment she "leaves her home at eighteen" and before she has had a chance to either fall into saving hands or "become worse" by assuming a foreign "standard of virtue." Dreiser uses the train ride into Chicago to establish both Carrie's characteristic mood and, in a sketchy yet telling way, the origins of her personality. At eighteen this country girl has passions and inner conflicts that are not at all simple. There is, in fact, much that Carrie is not conscious of in her feelings and motivations – an element of unconscious desire and wish that Dreiser underscores by surrounding her journey into Chicago with language taken from the imagery of dreams and of urban myths going back to Sodom and Gommorah. Carrie's path will be crossed "by forces wholly superhuman"; and, as if to signal the end of her adolescence, she enters the city at "that mystic period between the glare and the gloom of the world when life is changing from one sphere or condition to another" (10).

Carrie's deepest unconscious desires, before she is exposed to the "cunning wiles" of the city, partake of "wild dreams of some vague, far-off supremacy which should make it [the city] prey and subject, the proper penitent, grovelling at a woman's slipper" (4). The city as a subject of conquest, in her fantasies projected as a male figure, foreshadows the punishing side of her relations with men – just as her feelings of inferiority at the glitter of Drouet's presence suggest the equally strong sense of unworthiness in her personality. With her wild dreams of conquest remaining below the surface of consciousness, she comes to Chicago with certain conventional ends in mind: a new home, a life with her sister Minnie, and a job.

Instead she meets Drouet, who tempts her with flattery, with his purse and greenbacks, with sexual overtures; and Carrie begins to "drift" as his "luring" succeeds. On the train, Drouet accidentally calls up one of her most painful memories of home. When he mentions the names of the Columbia City merchants Morgenroth and Gibson, Carrie is "aroused by memories of longings the displays in the latter's establishment had cost her" (7). Full of light and color, Drouet can dispel Carrie's unhappy mood. But not for long. When she notices his clothes, she "became conscious of an inequality . . . [of being] shabby. She felt the worn state of her shoes." When the drummer mentions some of the major sights in Chicago, she senses an "ache in her fancy of all he described" and she feels her "insignificance in the presence of so much magnificence" (7). Though they are "both unconscious of how articulate all their real feelings were," they are sensitive to the sexual undercurrent between them. Drouet is no Ames, however, and from the start he misses Carrie's deeper emotion. As he continues to expand on the wonder of Chicago, Carrie shuts out his words:

> She did not hear this very well. Her heart was troubled by a kind of terror. The fact that she was alone, away from home, rushing into a great sea of life and endeavor began to tell. She could not help but feel a little choked for breath – a little sick as her heart beat so fast. (10)

Terror, large inhibitions, a sense of her insignificance along with unconscious dreams of conquest, memories of unsatisfied needs, psychosomatic symptoms, sudden mood swings – all these Carrie brings to Chicago with her, a figure whose unconscious yearnings and fearful temperament will determine the city's effect upon her.

Carrie's fears on the train are extreme, but they have a realistic component. Dreiser's method of exploring the inner world of his characters is to draw realistic surface tensions that, as in a Rembrandt portrait, point to more irrational elements below the surface. Carrie's panic attack passes when she meets her sister at the station, but it is replaced by other, more primal anxieties. For Carrie, Minnie "carried with her much of the grimness of shift and toil" (11). In contrast to Drouet, Minnie recalls the life she had left behind, and Carrie finds that "she was very much alone" with her sister, "a lone figure in a tossing, thoughtless sea" (12). Carrie's response brings to life Dreiser's first, rather abstract comment on her inner life. She was, he stresses, "not conscious" that the "threads which bound her so lightly to girlhood and home were irretrievably broken" (3).

Dreiser was acutely aware of the implications of this condition. The scene with Minnie at the end of Chapter 1 dramatizes beautifully what he explains with a heavier hand a few chapters later. There he traces the effect of Hurstwood's home life on his state of mind: the manager lacks a "lovely home atmosphere" which makes "strong and just the natures cradled and nurtured within it." In language that echoes the imagery used to explain Carrie's relation to her family, Dreiser concludes that those who miss this nurturing never know the "mystic cords which bind and thrill the heart." Those, like Carrie, for whom the cords don't bind very strongly, have been denied the family's "tolerance and love" and as a result "The song and the literature of the home are dulled" (81). The language is full of the sentimental clichés of the day, but it points to the hidden drama behind Carrie's first "perfunctory embrace" of Minnie on the train platform. "Sending back the shadow of a smile," Drouet leaves, smugly aware that for Carrie the conscious domestic ties are in conflict with more primitive and anarchic drives.

Carrie quickly begins to think of Minnie's place on West Van

Buren street as "home" (65), and with good reason, since it is for her an urban version of Columbia City. She soon feels about the Hanson flat what she feels about her old home: "Columbia City – what was there for her? She knew its dull little round by heart. . . . Now to turn back on it and live the little old life out there – she almost exclaimed against it as she thought" (65). She had left Wisconsin because she was "dissatisfied at home" (15), but life with her sister only revives "the old Carrie of distress." Dreiser makes Carrie's first period in Chicago duplicate her past life of deprivation, and so gives us a concrete sense of the roots of Carrie's psychic life without actually portraying (as he would for his second fictional "sister," Jennie Gerhardt) the specifics of her early life. He thereby collapses the conventional dichotomy between the provinces and the city found in the popular fiction of his day, and imposes a burden of psychological complexity on what has been described as "an old, old story: the restless country girl who comes to try her luck in the big city and never goes home again."[11]

What exactly do we know about Carrie's Wisconsin/Chicago family? Dreiser quietly conflates the characteristics of the two families, as he does Carrie's response to them. We learn that her father works in a flour mill, and that they are relative newcomers to Columbia City (and America). Carrie is "two generations removed from the emigrant" (4). Her father is therefore of the same generation as Sven Hanson, who, as the son of a Swedish father, still spoke English with "a certain Swedish accent, noticeable in his voice" (13). Of "a morbid turn of character," the silent, gloomy Hanson takes Carrie in mainly for financial relief, though the fiction of family bonds is perfunctorily observed. Like the Hansons, the Meebers are not settled economically, nor do they have deep ties to any place: "Once the family had thought of moving [to Chicago]. If she secured good employment they might come now" (3).

We also know that Carrie's early home life did not provide her with the guiding voice of a "counselor . . . to whisper cautious interpretations" (4). The guiding voice of the family – the counselor, traditionally the father's voice – is conspicuously absent in Carrie's life. Hanson does nothing to change this situation. He perpetuates the role of a parent who offers no careful direction to the young girl, playing instead on her sense of inadequacy. Dreiser stresses that Carrie is an easy mark for Drouet's early seductive advances because she "had no excellent home principles fixed upon her. If she had, she would have been more consciously distressed" (78). She hasn't even routine conventional "habits" to fall back on: "If any habits had ever had time to fix upon her, they would have operated here" (77). Dreiser thus links Carrie's weak sense of identity and her lack of a strong inner censor – and consequently her "fall" – to this early lack of guidance.

Because she had no early parental mentor "Her conscience . . . was no just and sapient counsellor" (89). Carrie's conscience only expresses the weak "voice of the people" which for her "was truly the voice of God" (89). Carrie's conscience proves to be no match for "the voice of want." When conscience speaks to her before the mirror at Drouet's flat, she argues with herself: "What else could I do? I was so bad off. Where could I have gone? Not home again – oh, I did not want to go there." In answer, her conscience orders her to return: "Step into the streets, return to your home, be as you were. Escape!' 'I can't. I can't,' was her only reply" (91).

Carrie's dread of returning home is connected to certain key memories. Her sensitivity to the poor and downtrodden – as well as her own fear of that fate – stems from mixed feelings of pity and shame over her father's lot in life. The streets call up many associations that center on a recurring memory.

> Her old father, in his flour-dusted miller's suit, sometimes returned to her in memory – revived by a face in the window. A shoemaker pegging at his last, a blastman seen through a narrow window in some basement where iron was being melted, a bench worker seen high aloft in some window, his coat off, his sleeves up – these took her back in fancy to the details of the mill. She felt, though she seldom expressed them, sad thoughts upon this score. Her sympathies were ever with the underworld of toil from which she had so recently sprung and which she best understood. (146–7)

There is, then, a division in Carrie that suggests some of the earliest sources of her conflicts and depressions. She both identifies with and seeks to flee "the underworld of toil from which she had so recently sprung." Her sympathies spring from her identification; but her melancholy comes from a sense of shame which follows her through the city streets, where conscience nags but is no match for the intense fears which stem from the thought that she herself might end that way. "She would stand and bite her lips" at the sight of poorly clad girls and "the white-faced, ragged men who slopped desperately by her in a sort of mental stupor" (145).

Carrie's unresolved tensions, based upon painful memories of her childhood, are most apparent in her relations with men. She measures their worth in direct proportion to their ability to provide her with the food, shelter, clothing, and pleasures that were missing during her early years. It was the "nature of her longings," Dreiser reminds us at the end of the novel, that alone explains Drouet's and Hurstwood's "influence on her life" (369 N). Carrie's noted lack of passion with men is the result of her desire to satisfy more basic needs than the sexual. Her fears and insecurities make the free play of sexual love impossible for her, as she seeks from men what she lacked at home – and takes out on them her guilty anger at what she recurrently experiences as abandonment. As a result, Carrie's first concern is for her immediate needs. Yet her narcissistic self-involvement is primarily neither that of the golddigger nor of the incipient artist but of a woman whose deprived childhood made the fear of further want her strongest emotion.[12]

It is appropriate, then, that Carrie's initial temptation is imagined as a tension between seducer and family. Minnie's first question at the train station, " 'Why, how are all the folks at home' – she began – 'how is Father, and Mother?' " (11) is "answered," but we do not hear the answer. Instead we see Carrie looking away from her sister toward Drouet: "When he disappeared she felt his absence thoroughly" (12). Drouet's presence brings a new "atmosphere" into Carrie's life, one that is contrasted with the more usual depressive feelings she associates with her family. In this way Dreiser taps the unconscious yearnings and fears in Carrie, as he begins the story of a waif who was not "cradled a child of fortune." The language of cradling and nurturing is not fortuitous. Dreiser understood the implications of Carrie's upbringing and made it memorable in the image readers recall most often: Carrie's incessant rocking in her chair, a classic symptom of those who are not nurtured and made to feel secure in early childhood.[13]

Carrie flees from the Hansons as she would from her parents. "'Sven doesn't think it looks good to stand there,' [Minnie] said. 'Doesn't he?' said Carrie. 'I wouldn't do it any more after this' " (72). With her letter, she defies and breaks with the stern father and with the sympathetic but helpless mother. Carrie always leaves furtively, irretrievably breaking all bonds, because her primary relation to home and family is full of rebellion and shame. However passive in personal encounters, Carrie has the capacity for "mental rebellion" (55) which she directs toward her new home as well as toward Columbia City.

Her flight from the Hansons continues the pattern that began with her leaving Wisconsin and that also continues in her domestic relations with men. Finally she leaves them, as she left her family, with pity in the memory of them and guilt in the leaving – and with the inability to be anything but lightly bound to anyone. After she goes to live with Drouet, she one day passes the Hanson flat: "She could see it through some open lots, the front curtains half drawn. Minnie was in the kitchen getting supper. For a moment Carrie winced perceptibly. It was like a slap in the face" (101). Yet she could not return: of the surrogate father figure of Sven "She knew she did not like him" – a feeling she comes to have for all the men in her life. Years after she leaves Drouet, she remains "ashamed of her conduct" (436). In her last relationship, with Hurstwood, she relives the Hanson – and family – situation of want: "Her mind went back to her early venture in Chicago, the Hansons and their flat, and her heart revolted" (345). Once more she leaves a note and flees guiltily. When she decides to leave, it is not only with a sense of self-justification; again "she felt very much like a criminal in the matter" (435).

Carrie's need for men always includes marriage and reflects her desire for respectability as well as for security. She is in fact rather obsessive on this point.[14] When she does "marry," it is to a man whose daughter is her age. There is "no great passion in her" for Hurstwood, but unlike Drouet he agrees to Carrie's major demand: "You must marry me" (301). Such is the intensity of her desire that she blocks out the fact of his bigamy, a repression that Hurstwood (as well as many readers) finds hard to believe. But the strength of her underlying needs – "for the first time in her life she felt settled and somewhat justified in the eyes of society" (313) – again take us back to the anxieties of Columbia City.

Columbia City chose to define (and limit) Caroline Meeber in a very specific way: "'Sister Carrie,' as she had been half affectionately termed by the family" (4). There is in the title of the book a clue to the fate of its heroine. As Carrie's passions are for those things that she dreamed of finding at home, so family relations shape her story. To be a "kept" woman for Carrie is to be in the position of a daughter who is "half affectionately" called "sister." She is poorly kept at the Hansons by her real sister, then goes to Drouet, who is a "brotherly sort of creature in his demeanor" (60) and who proclaims his triumph in terms that appeal to Carrie: "Now you're my sister" (70). Minnie announces Carrie's departure to Sven with the elegant "Sister Carrie has gone to live somewhere else" (74). The familial locution here has a formal ring to it. It declares that Carrie is carrying her conflicted sisterhood beyond the confines of Columbia City and the Hansons to all the figures and places in the novel – to Drouet, to Hurstwood, and finally to the chorus line and the theater. At the end, Carrie's presence is felt not so much as lover, friend, or even actress, but as a dependent sister.

3

Among *Sister Carrie*'s most famous scenes is Carrie's acting debut in Augustus Daly's melodrama *Under the Gaslight*. Carrie plays Laura, a girl her own age who is threatened with banishment from society when it is discovered that she is really the daughter of riffraff. Carrie assumes the role with a moving sympathy that surprises everyone, including herself. In manuscript Dreiser prepared for this moment by establishing the theater as the arena where one enters the realm of dream and the unconscious. It would, he says, "require the pen of a Hawthorne . . . to do justice to that mingled atmosphere of life and mummery" that Carrie was experiencing. Such a world breathes "of the other half of life in which we have no part, of doors that are closed, and mysteries which may never be revealed" (176).

Within this world of mysteries, Carrie finds a voice. Laura is,

Dreiser tells us, a character full of "suffering and tears" (160), and Carrie finds in the sentimental plight of Daly's heroine a mirror of her own aspirations and fears.[15] "This part affected Carrie deeply. It reminded her somehow of her own state" (163). At the time, Carrie is being courted by Hurstwood, whose social position "affected her much as the magnificence of God affects the mind of the Christian" (129). During the performance, Carrie enters imaginatively into the part only after Laura is threatened with a return to that underworld of toil from which she came and is rejected by her lover – "the society individual who was to waiver in his thoughts of marrying her, upon finding that she was a waif and a nobody by birth" (167). After her nervous start in the opening scenes, Carrie suddenly brings the part to life as she "began to feel the bitterness of the situation. The feelings of the outcast descended upon her" (184).

Laura's nightmare, with its source in the discovery of her family origins, is realized when she is brought to court for disobedience to her supposed father. On stage Carrie becomes, in the fancy of her role, "some beggar's child" (162). Because Dreiser intended *Under the Gaslight* to function as a "play within a play," that is, as an index to Carrie's real-life drama, he transfers the climax of Daly's play to the fourth act; and he skips over the fact that the last act of pure melodrama – complete with a train track rescue – shows Laura to be the real insider and her cousin Pearl the actual beggar's daughter. "In a few minutes, the last act [V] was over" (193) is all the notice Dreiser gives of the play's real finale. It is Carrie's identification with the Laura who is abandoned by society and family that defines her ability as an artist of the pathetic.

In Daly's play the fantasy is that such a character has the power and nobility to give up her respectable lover, Ray. The climax of Carrie's role comes in a scene where Laura sublimates her own fears and desires with an impassioned and self-aggrandizing speech to Ray about the true love of a "virtuous lady": "when misfortune and evil have defeated your greatest purposes – her love remains to console you . . . love is all a woman has to give . . . " (192). Carrie can feel on stage the selfless love she can never feel in real life. Her unconscious desires breathe life into the melodramatic role of Laura, so that she moves her real offstage lovers to believe, for the first and only time, that she is speaking to them from the heart.

Although we never see Carrie in another major role, her stage successes are all charged with this sort of emotional transference. "If you wish to be merry, see Carrie's frown" (448) reads one of her first newspaper notices. Carrie's blues are the source of her appeal and of the particular chemistry she arouses in the audience, even in popular comedy. An opportunity comes in the role of "a silent little Quakeress"; though Carrie has no lines, her demeanor captivates the audience, partly through its comic incongruity to the stage burlesque. But her frown also expresses that mixture of coyness and dependence that had attracted Drouet and Hurstwood: "It was the kind of frown [men] would have loved to force away with kisses. All the gentlemen yearned towards her" (447).

If, as critics have noted, Dreiser modeled Carrie's meteoric stage success partly on the career of his brother Paul Dresser, then the wide mood swings that afflicted Paul surely contributed to his portrait of Carrie.[16] Dreiser associated Carrie's (and Paul's) creativity less with extraordinary talent or intellectual insight than with an "emotional greatness" that gives imaginative expression to the world's common sorrows. As a type of "one who feels, rather than reasons" (369 N), Carrie exhibits a melancholy which is, in this scheme, a function of her creative sensibility: "The thing in her that could sink and sink and make her feel depressed was a finer mental strain" (69). Carrie's ability to see "glimpses of the misery of things" becomes, within the course of the novel, the quality that defines the heart of the artistic personality.

Given what little we see of Carrie's talents, the seriousness Dreiser brings to his romantic portrait of her as an "artist" is unconvincing. Since we never see Carrie advance to the point where she takes Ames's advice to enter the "dramatic field," her growth in sensibility is measured less by her acting than by her response to the works of Hardy and Balzac that Ames recommends. The final scene with Carrie finds her absorbed in *Père Goriot,* aware of the worthlessness of her early reading. When she chides Lola Osborne for thinking of sleigh riding during the snowstorm, Carrie gives us the only clue to her interest in the book: "'Oh dear,' said Carrie, with whom the sufferings of father Goriot were still keen. 'That's all you think of. Aren't you sorry for the people who haven't got anything tonight'" (495). Instead of identifying with Eugene de Rastignac, her counterpart in Balzac's novel, Carrie broods over the fate of Goriot. Goriot ends his days in destitution and goes to his grave unattended by his daughters, who send servants in their place. Given Carrie's memories of her father and the sad thoughts they evoke, the sufferings of Goriot naturally touch her. But her sad thoughts remain just that, and she sits fixed in her familiar posture, unable to move beyond her brooding meditations. While Hurstwood goes unattended to his grave, Carrie lives out her old "wild dreams of . . . supremacy"; and in leaving him she, like Laura in Daly's play, escapes the pain of being a "beggar's child."

Carrie pays a price for this freedom: insofar as she brings these motives into her relations with men, Carrie perpetuates the conflicts of her childhood. In manuscript Dreiser developed Carrie's flirtation with Ames to the brink of a possible union. The two meet again when Carrie has achieved all she most desired: She has a new "sister" in Lola; an anonymous provider who indulges her with a new "home" at the Waldorf; and in Ames a new "lover" from the West whose guiding voice of counsel offers her cautious interpretations of the world she faces. Ames is, in fact, the sort of man Carrie might marry if she were able to free herself of her neurosis and enter into a satisfying relationship. Dreiser wisely heeded Arthur Henry's advice and resisted that solution to Carrie's problems. A consummated relation with Ames would have destroyed the inner logic of Carrie's character and created a melodramatic resolution in the spirit of *Under the Gaslight*. Instead, Dreiser leaves Carrie wondering whether "such a man as he would [ever] care to draw nearer" (487); and in fact answers her doubts in the epilogue, where he assures us that, even had she succeeded with Ames, there "would lie others for her" (369 N). She remains, in short, "the old mournful Carrie – the desireful Carrie, – unsatisfied."

Carrie's story, then, is only partially one of material and artistic rise.[17] There is also the downward drag of spiritual decline that inhabits all of Dreiser's novels, and that is captured in *Sister Carrie* by Hurstwood's final "What's the use?" – the line that ends the novel in manuscript. This downward pull fills the novel with a depressive air that attends even Carrie's final stage triumph. Hearing the applause of celebrity, she still feels "mildly guilty of something – perhaps unworthiness" (450). That her depression remains after she has attained more than she desired in the way of material goods and fame points to Dreiser's major theme. "She had learned that in his [Hurstwood's] world, as in her own present state, was not happiness" (369 N). Hurstwood's "What's the use?" is echoed in the epilogue, where Dreiser uses his own charged rhetoric to express his inarticulate heroine's feelings: "Know, then, that for you is neither surfeit nor content. In your rocking-chair, by your window dreaming, shall you long, alone. In your rocking-chair, by your window, shall you dream such happiness as you may never feel" (369 N). Dreiser voices Carrie's longings and fears at the end, as her lament of loneliness, sadness, hopeless struggle and isolation, of evil forces at work in the world – the feelings, that is, of an anxious child – dominate the final pages.

In these pages Dreiser invites us to share Carrie's sorrow by identifying it with the condition of the world itself. The origin of this impulse is Dreiser's own depressive temperament, which in his work and in his life he made persistent attempts to evade or, as in the epilogue to *Sister Carrie,* to find relief from in philosophy. Despite his fictional preference for sisters, financiers, and unimaginative sons of weak parents, Dreiser was a consistently autobiographical writer, and Carrie no less than Eugene Witla is partly a vehicle to explore his own psychic life. Dreiser was prone to identify the conflicts of his own inner world with the way of the world at large. He invested his first heroine with his own somber view of the nature of things. Yet he gave her not just his perplexities but the capacities he himself banked on for personal salvation. Emotionally maimed as she is, Carrie has the ability to "dream" and to "hope." Yet at the end her more basic and darker inner convictions have been confirmed: she is stripped of the illusion that happiness could be found in men or material goods – or even in fame as an artist. The resolution, such as it is, is not to move outward into the world but to rock in the chair, a kind of perpetual circular motion that brings back the old, mournful self essentially unaltered by knowledge or experience.

Like her creator in 1900, Carrie is pre-Freudian, and her motives remain something of a mystery to her. "Oh, the tangle of human life! How dimly as yet we see" (454). Even the sage advice of Ames – an extension of the wise voice of the narrator – cannot alter the inner person. In effect, Dreiser made Carrie's main adversary the melancholic part of her own mind. But he could find no way of relieving her sufferings. In the epilogue, he challenges the exterior causes of gloom – her physical and material needs; and he re-directs our focus to less tangible yearnings, like the pursuit of beauty and the unsatisfied hunger of the imagination, that provide appropriate metaphors for Carrie's melancholic state of mind.

The authorial voice – in a way the fourth main character in the book – remains in the position of Carrie at the end; figuratively speaking, he sits in his rocking chair with *Père Goriot* in his lap, rocking and dreaming, as he applies philosophical balm to Carrie's wounds – wounds that are contiguous with the world as he imag-ines it. At the close of the published novel, the intrusion of the narrator in the epilogue, florid and strained as it is, allows Dreiser to bring us back to the repressed and confused Carrie in all her easeful melancholy. After our trip with Hurstwood, ending in the despair of his final moments, the blue dreamer in her rocking chair is a great relief.

NOTES

1. William Marion Reedy, "Sister Carrie," St. Louis *Mirror*, 10 (January 3, 1901); 6–7. Reprinted in *Critical Essays on Theodore Dreiser*, ed. Donald Pizer (Boston: G. K. Hall, 1981), p. 158.

2. Anonymous, New York *Commercial Advertiser*, December 19, 1900. Reprinted in *Theodore Dreiser: The Critical Reception*, ed. Jack Salzman (New York: David Lewis, 1972), p. 4.

3. For a good sample of the early reviews of *Sister Carrie*, see Salzman, *The Critical Reception*, pp. 1–54.

4. *Sister Carrie*, eds. John C. Berkey, James L. W. West III, Neda M. Westlake, Alice M. Winters (Philadelphia: University of Pennsylvania Press, 1981), p. 145. I will quote from this edition because it captures Dreiser's rendering of Carrie's character at an earlier stage of composi-tion and therefore more fully than the first edition published by Dou-bleday, Page, the edition which is the basis for the text of the Norton

Critical Edition. I will also quote from the Norton Critical Edition, however, when I wish to cite a passage not in the Pennsylvania Edition. All citations from the Pennsylvania Edition will be followed in the text by page numbers in parentheses; all citations from the Norton Critical Edition will be followed in the text by page numbers and "N" in parentheses.

5. Ellen Moers, *Two Dreisers* (New York: Viking, 1969), p. 107.

6. F. O. Matthiessen, *Theodore Dreiser* (New York: William Sloane Associates, 1951), p. 85.

7. For recent, provocative treatments of this theme, see Philip Fisher, "The Life History of Objects: The Naturalist Novel and the City," in *Hard Facts* (New York: Oxford University Press, 1985), pp. 153–78; Amy Kaplan, "The Sentimental Revolt of *Sister Carrie*," in *The Social Construction of American Realism* (Chicago: University of Chicago Press, 1988), pp. 140–60; and Walter Benn Michaels, "*Sister Carrie*'s Popular Economy," in *The Gold Standard and the Logic of Naturalism* (Berkeley: University of California Press, 1987), pp. 29–58.

8. Among the few critics to address the question, Kenneth S. Lynn shrewdly focuses on Carrie's "depressed, dissatisfied" personality. Lynn argues that these symptoms reflect the pathology of the gold digger, and he concludes that "Dreiser's instinctive knowledge of his heroine led him to describe quite accurately an attitude of mind which he did not consciously understand." ("Theodore Dreiser: The Man of Ice," in *The Dream of Success* [Boston: Little Brown and Company, 1955], p. 34.) Carrie does, of course, have something of the gold digger about her, as is often the case with this type of personality.

9. Ellen Moers, "The Finesse of Dreiser," *American Scholar* 33 (Winter, 1964): 109–14; reprinted in Pizer, *Critical Essays*, p. 201.

10. Moers, *Two Dreisers*, p. 100.

11. Ibid., p. 99.

12. The connection between an emotionally deprived childhood and narcissism is discussed in Alice Miller, *Prisoners of Childhood: The Drama of the Gifted Child and the Search for the True Self*, trans. by Ruth Ward (New York: Basic Books, 1981).

13. For discussions of this condition see "Stereotypy/Habits Disorder," in *Diagnostic and Statistical Manual of Mental Disorders*, ed. Robert L. Spitzer, third edition revised (Washington, D. C.: American Psychiatric Association: 1987), pp. 93–5; and Harry Harlow, *Determinants of Infant Behaviour* (London: Methuen, 1961), p. 89. I am in debt to Dr. Robert Catenaccio for leading me to these sources and for the many hours of discussion about Dreiser and other matters over the years. For different

views of Carrie's rocking, see Donald Pizer, *"Sister Carrie,"* in *The Novels of Theodore Dreiser* (Minneapolis: University of Minnesota Press, 1976), pp. 67, 82; and Philip Fisher, *Hard Facts*, pp. 154–6.

14. For a good discussion of Carrie's "domesticity," see Kaplan, *Social Construction of American Realism*, pp. 144–5.
15. See Donald Pizer's discussion of Dreiser's use of *Under the Gaslight* in *Novels of Theodore Dreiser*, pp. 41–2.
16. The best analysis of Paul Dresser's emotional instability is in Richard Lingeman, *Theodore Dreiser: At the Gates of the City, 1871–1907* (New York; Putnam's, 1986), pp. 392–6.
17. Warwick Wadlington makes a strong case for the existence in Carrie of a "core of innate psychic activity that exists buried in all [Dreiser's] characters, rising fitfully, 'opportunistically' to the surface only when an external reality seems to promise fulfillment," in "Pathos and Dreiser," *Southern Review* 7 (Spring 1971): 411–29; reprinted in Pizer, *Critical Essays*, p. 222.

A Portrait of the Artist as a Young Actress: The Rewards of Representation in *Sister Carrie* *

BARBARA HOCHMAN

T HE history of *Sister Carrie* has long been informed by contradictory, sometimes apocryphal accounts of the novel's composition and publication.[1] When asked about his work on *Sister
Carrie*, Dreiser himself tended to stress the "mystic" component in
his writing process. He often described his sense of having been
"used . . . like a medium,"[2] when he wrote the first words of the
text, and of finishing the manuscript with the help of "inspiration"
that came "suddenly . . . of its own accord."[3]

While writing *Sister Carrie*, however, Dreiser evolved certain
habits of composition which significantly complicate the image of
autonomous inspiration that he later fostered. Like Carrie's first
public appearance on stage, Dreiser's first attempt to write a novel
was facilitated by the intensive mediation of other people. Indeed,
the sustained involvement of friends, lovers, readers, and editors
was indispensable to Dreiser's fiction writing all his life.[4]

Dreiser's long-standing emphasis on his solitary moments of creative inspiration is especially interesting in the context of the collaborative process that informed the composition of *Sister Carrie*.[5]
Throughout that process, Dreiser's wife, Jug, and his friend Arthur
Henry made myriad suggestions, emendations, and excisions,

I would like to thank Emory Elliott and the National Endowment for the
Humanities for the chance to participate in a Summer Seminar on History
and American Fiction, where many of the ideas for this essay began to
germinate.

*Throughout this chapter I use the term *representation* to suggest, not the
imitation of an objective reality, but rather the expressive impulse as it seeks
articulation, especially in front of others, whether in words, in music, or in
person.

large and small. In addition, they (and especially Henry) repeatedly helped Dreiser resist the temptation to abandon the manuscript altogether. Not only did Dreiser rely on this assistance, he often took an active pleasure in it. "If [Henry] had been a girl I would have married him, of course," he once said.[6]

Dreiser's accounts of inspired creativity, calculated in part to attract the attention of readers (both to his work and to himself),[7] also serve to dramatize the writer's alleged independence. While Dreiser's autobiographical vignettes would seem to make him personally accessible to the public at large, they simultaneously assert not only the writer's own radical autonomy but even his ontological otherness.

Both Dreiser's stake in creative autonomy and his need for editorial and moral support are clearly reflected in his rendering of Carrie's unfolding career as an actress. Many of Dreiser's first newspaper sketches explore the conditions that facilitate the work of the aspiring artist; other early pieces depict the satisfactions of success.[8] In *Sister Carrie,* however, Dreiser engages a wider range of issues implicit in his conception of artistic performance.

Through the figure of Carrie, Dreiser projects a version of his personal experience as a writer. His rendering of Carrie, especially on stage and backstage, dramatizes both the intricacies of an artist's relationship with his or her audience (whether readers or spectators) and the complexities inherent in the act of representation itself. Carrie's story also reveals the dynamic through which, as Dreiser sees it, the artist gains access to his or her own sources of vitality or "inspiration." Thus when Carrie plays Laura in *Under the Gaslight,* she may be taken as a stand-in for the figure of the writer, desperately in need of encouragement and support. At the same time, however, Dreiser's rendering of Carrie in this sequence reflects his conviction that, under certain conditions, the performing (and perhaps the fiction-writing) self may have access to a range of satisfactions unavailable in any other context.

Dreiser's own experience while writing *Sister Carrie,* like Carrie's experience on stage in Chicago and New York, ran the gamut from a sense of unique communion with a small but responsive group of supporters, to a sense of isolation – even betrayal – after publication of the novel. Like Dreiser in the course of composition,

Carrie in *Under the Gaslight* performs most effectively (and feels most gratified) when the process of representation is accompanied by immediate response and collaborative support from intimate spectators.

Carrie never again acts as well as she does in that volunteer amateur production of *Under the Gaslight,* for which the patronage of Hurstwood insures a well-disposed, good-natured audience, and during which part of the audience ends up on the other side of the footlights. Only when Drouet comes backstage after the feeble first scene to "buoy [Carrie] up" (134)[9] in her efforts does Carrie gain access to her full creative energy. In the course of the novel, moreover, Carrie becomes increasingly "professional," and her audience increasingly distant. As her isolation increases, the rewards of the dramatic enterprise progressively diminish. By the time Carrie resides in the Waldorf, at the end of the book, the vibrant image of Drouet backstage, buoying Carrie up, has been replaced by a barrage of letters from strangers, more or less bidding to "buy" her. Only her final encounter with Robert Ames recalls the responsive support that once allowed her to realize the full power and pleasure of her gift.

Her performance in *Under the Gaslight* is probably the closest thing to "happiness" that Carrie ever knows. The role of Laura stirs her deepest feelings. Virtuous and self-effacing, Laura seems precisely what Carrie is not. Yet Carrie identifies wholeheartedly with certain aspects of this figure – poor orphan and outcast, forlorn in the big city. For Carrie to "be" Laura in this sense involves both a dramatization of what she takes to be her own state, and an identification with radical otherness.[10]

In Augustin Daly's melodrama, virtue is amply rewarded before the final curtain. Laura, who has been ready to sacrifice everything, ultimately wins back not only her man and her money, but her standing in society and her brightest expectations for the future. This happy ending, however, is nowhere suggested in Dreiser's own text. Thus Carrie's Laura, stoically facing her difficulties, remains a poignant figure of loss – while Carrie herself becomes a "medium" for what Robert Ames later calls "the [world's] sorrows and longing" (356; cf. 485 Penn).

It is in the act of embodying loss, however, that Carrie experiences her greatest satisfactions. Carrie's representational gift thus emerges from the text as a complex and paradoxical quality. Carrie's talent, like Dreiser's, is her most negotiable asset; it catapults her into a position of celebrity and wealth. Yet it is at the same time the source of satisfactions that, from Dreiser's point of view, are indeed (as the heroine in *Under the Gaslight* says of love) "without price" (139).

When Carrie "dawn[s] . . . upon the audience, handsome and proud . . . moving forward with a steady grace, born of inspiration" (135), she is oblivious to other actors and audience alike. It is a unique moment in Carrie's experience. Her histrionic talent affords her both a passionate sense of human connectedness and an incomparable thrill of independence. Later her talent makes money for Carrie even while seeming to offer her escape, not only from the pervasive conditions of the marketplace but from life in society altogether. It allows Carrie to represent otherness even while articulating her own personal "melancholy of desire."

Toward the end of the novel, Robert Ames speaks of Carrie's "natural expression" as the source of her histrionic power: To him, Carrie's face is "representative of all desire" (356). I will suggest that Carrie's first triumph as an actress derives not only from her capacity to articulate desire through her histrionic gift but also from her capacity to engage in a collaborative interaction with spectators. Before examining Carrie's first performance in detail, however, I will argue that throughout *Sister Carrie,* the act of representation is seen to have its sources in desire and its greatest satisfaction in a process that begins in collaboration – even dependency – but that ultimately affords the self a euphoric if short-lived experience of soaring autonomy.

The text of *Sister Carrie* is pervaded by references to the multiple forms of desire – "the craving for pleasure" (24), the "constant drag to something better" (77), "the siren voice of the unrestful" (86). Since fulfillment of desire (in any form) is far less frequent, however, such satisfaction as characters do achieve seems to warrant particular attention.

One of Carrie's first guides to the pleasures of the city is her neighbor in Chicago, Mrs. Hale. "Mrs. Hale loved to drive in the afternoon in the sun when it was fine, and to satisfy her soul with a sight of those mansions and lawns which she could not afford" (86). How, one might ask, does the sight of what Mrs. Hale lacks – "those mansions and lawns which she could not afford" – come to "satisfy her soul"?

In order to derive satisfaction from the sight of what she lacks, Mrs. Hale would seem to project herself imaginatively into the mansions that she contemplates from a distance. Like Carrie, who accompanies her on one of her carriage rides, Mrs. Hale presumably "imagine[s] . . . that across these richly carved entrance-ways . . . set with stained and designed panes of glass, was neither care nor unsatisfied desire" (86). Thus the representing imagination, conjuring up its objects of desire, turns those imagined objects into grounds of satisfaction. Throughout the text of *Sister Carrie*, Carrie's own insatiable longings, amorphous but urgent, are the mainspring of her histrionic gift. Here, like Carrie in her rocking chair, Mrs. Hale transforms potential pain (wishing, but not having) into satisfaction via the process of representation.

This maneuver is repeated and elaborated when Carrie returns to her room after her outing, "the glow of the palatial doors . . . still in her eye, the roll of cushioned carriages still in her ears" (87). The excursion has struck a responsive chord in Carrie's susceptible imagination; but Carrie's longings are more pervasive as well as more diffuse than Mrs. Hale's. Rocking near her window, she

> longed and longed and longed. It was now for the old cottage room in Columbia City, now the mansion upon the Shore Drive, now the fine dress of some lady, now the elegance of some scene. She was sad beyond measure. . . . Finally, it seemed as if all her state was one of forsakenness, and she could scarce refrain from trembling at the lip. She hummed and hummed as the moments went by, sitting in the shadow by the window, and was therein as happy, though she did not perceive it, as ever she would be. (87)

Unlike Mrs. Hale, whose "satisfaction" implicitly derives from her imagined claim upon inaccessible mansions and lawns, Carrie proliferates objects of unfulfillable desire, until the condition of longing itself becomes the ground of satisfaction. By evoking what she lacks until "it seemed as if all her state was one of loneliness and forsakenness" Carrie enters a state of forlornness that the narrative voice directly equates with happiness.

If Carrie's sadness, rocking and humming, makes her "as happy . . . as ever she would be," however, one might yet ask why she herself "did not perceive" her own happiness here, and what would enable her to do so. An earlier scene of Carrie's rocking helps clarify this point. In Chapter 11, when the "wistful [piano] chords" of another neighbor "aw[a]ke longings [in Carrie] for those things which she did not have" (77), Carrie's melancholy musings recall her "to the . . . saddest [things] within the small limit of her experience" (78). At this point Drouet enters, bringing with him an "entirely different atmosphere," and proceeding to make the "incongruous proposition" that they "waltz a little to that music." It is "his first great mistake" with Carrie (78).

Drouet's abrupt intrusion serves to short-circuit Carrie's melancholy satisfactions. While Carrie may not fully perceive her own happiness when she indulges her reflections alone, the mood is transformed into outright irritation when interrupted by an unempathic observer. No spectator at all would seem to be better than one who fails to harmonize with Carrie's current of feeling. When Mrs. Hale invites Carrie to participate in her carriage ride, she is well aware that Carrie has awakened "in the matter of desire" (86). Thus she implicitly assumes that Carrie will support rather than undercut her own responses to mansions and lawns.

If Drouet fails Carrie by misreading her mood when he finds her rocking sadly in the dusk, he more than makes up for it when Carrie plays Laura in *Under the Gaslight*. Both during rehearsals and on opening night, Drouet is enthusiastically supportive and receptive – in short, the perfect audience. Drouet's role in this sequence is crucial, not only in helping Carrie to realize her dramatic potential, but also in enabling her to recognize – and thus delight in – her achievement. It is as if a collaborating presence were indispensable not only for eliciting creative energy, but also for reflecting the pleasure of success back to the uncertain artist. Thus the lack of a spectator partially explains Carrie's failure to perceive her own happiness when she sits alone in her rocking chair.[11]

Fittingly, it is on stage (even more than in her rocking chair) that

Carrie experiences her most rewarding and passionate moments. The process of imaginative representation is repeatedly seen to create a sense of fulfillment, however short-lived, even while it facilitates the expression of desire. Indeed, as I have suggested, for Carrie to embody desire through representation is already in a sense for her to satisfy it. But Carrie's satisfaction playing Laura in *Under the Gaslight* derives only in part from the process of representation itself; at Avery Hall those inherent rewards are substantially enhanced by the accompanying sense of contact between Carrie and her audience.

Carrie's performance as Laura constitutes a high point of satisfaction – hope, delight, emotional intensity – not only for Carrie but also for Hurstwood and Drouet.[12] It is not merely that Carrie never again acts as effectively as she does in this performance. It is also that in a world where human relations can almost invariably be reduced to buyer and seller, exploiter and exploited, or where, as Richard Poirier puts it, "sex [is] . . . almost the only imaginable form of personal interchange,"[13] the collaborative effort that culminates in Carrie's triumph on stage is a unique interaction, a rare coming together by characters whose general capacity to respond to the needs or desires of another person is virtually nil.

To be sure, Drouet, Hurstwood, and Carrie herself all approach the Elks project with a characteristic emphasis on their own self-interest. When Drouet suggests that Carrie take the part of Laura, it is simply "an easy way out" (115) of a troublesome obligation. Similarly, Hurstwood's efforts on behalf of her performance – both his original encouragement of Carrie and his effort to "make it a dress-suit affair and give the little girl a chance" (121) – stem largely from his determination to impress his irresistible qualities upon her, to benefit from her increasing regard. Nonetheless, given the generous measure of delusion, deceit, and self-interest that informs human relations throughout *Sister Carrie*, the motives and actions of these three characters during the *Under the Gaslight* sequence are surprisingly benign. It is a rare moment, for example, when Drouet ("this goodly drummer [who] carried the doom of all enduring relationships in his own lightsome manner and unstable fancy" [92]) is "really moved," as he is by Carrie's first tentative "excellent representation" of Laura in their flat (119). "Well, you're a wonder," Drouet tells her after she faints to the floor. "He had bounded up to catch her, and now held her laughing in his arms."

> "Ain't you afraid you'll hurt yourself?" he asked.
> "Not a bit."
> "Well, you're a wonder. Say, I never knew you could do anything like that."
> "I never did either," said Carrie merrily, her face flushed with delight.
> "Well, you can bet that you're all right," said Drouet. "You can take my word for that. You won't fail." (120)

This is a striking exchange. Such pleasurable contact between two characters is in itself rare enough in *Sister Carrie*. But the scene is unusual both as a rendering of mutual good feeling (even laughter!) and as a rare image of spontaneous encouragement and support offered with no strings attached. This support in turn reacts upon Carrie to enhance her own sense of achievement and possibility.

The entire *Under the Gaslight* sequence is informed by Carrie's need for encouragement, support, praise, feedback – now from Drouet, now from Hurstwood. Both men contribute significantly to Carrie's success. Her triumph is the result of a genuinely collaborative effort of the three. This effort may be taken as a model for what Dreiser conceived to be the ideal unfolding of artistic representation, culminating in the artist's momentary capacity to transcend not only the need for, but even the awareness of, all spectators.

The pattern is already evident in the scene just cited. When Drouet first asks Carrie to let him hear what she has practiced, Carrie hesitates. A bit of prodding by Drouet, however, enables Carrie to overcome her inhibitions and eventually to execute "the ball-room episode with considerable feeling, *forgetting, as she got deeper into the scene, all about Drouet, and letting herself rise to a fine state of feeling*" (119; my emphasis). Ironically, though Carrie cannot begin without Drouet's encouragement, her "fine state of feeling" depends upon her "forgetting . . . about Drouet" altogether. Moreover, her progressive indifference to Drouet makes her rendering of Laura, in turn, the more irresistible to him.

50

This pattern is repeated when Carrie plays Laura on opening night. Despite Hurstwood's patronage, which assures a large turn-out for the event (a "well-dressed, good-natured, flatteringly-in-clined audience was assured from the moment he thought of as-sisting Carrie" [127]), Carrie's performance in the first scene is devastatingly weak. It is only when Drouet goes backstage that she "revive[s] a little" (133). "[G]rateful for the drummer's presence, [Carrie] . . . tried to think she could do it" (133). Drouet, for his part, keeps up a steady stream of supportive chatter while Carrie waits in the wings for her cue. When the prompter signals, she begins to make her entrance, "weak as ever, but suddenly her nerve partially returned. She thought of Drouet looking" (133).

After the scene, Drouet is ready with praise and more encour-agement. Finally his efforts pay off: he "buoyed Carrie up most effectually."

> He began to make her feel as if she had done very well. The old melancholy of desire began to come back as he talked at her, and by the time the situation rolled round she was running high in feeling. . . .
>
> At the sound of her stage name Carrie started. She began to feel the bitterness of the situation. The feelings of the outcast descended upon her. She hung at the wing's edge, rapt in her own mounting thoughts. She hardly heard anything more, save her own rumbling blood.
>
> "Come girls!" said Mrs. Van Dam solemnly. . . .
>
> "Cue," said the prompter, close to her side, but she did not hear. Already she was moving forward with a steady grace, born of in-spiration. She dawned upon the audience, handsome and proud. . . .
>
> Hurstwood blinked his eyes and caught the infection. The radiat-ing waves of feeling and sincerity were already breaking against the farthest walls of the chamber. The magic of passion, which will yet dissolve the world, was here at work. (134–5)

This sequence reproduces the dialectical pattern of support and independence which was evident in the earlier scene between Drouet and Carrie. Drouet's supportive, coaxing, badgering pres-ence ultimately issues in Carrie's whole-hearted identification with her role. Momentarily transformed into Laura, the sound of "her stage name" makes her "start." Increasingly impervious not only to Drouet but to the prompter and the rest of the company, she is "rapt in her own mounting thoughts" and "hardly [hears] anything more."[14]

As a touchstone to what the narrative voice calls "the magic of passion which will yet dissolve the world," Carrie's experience as Laura is a climactic moment – the more so since romantic passion has no place in the world of *Sister Carrie*. Describing Hurstwood's infatuation with Carrie, the narrative voice notes that Hurstwood lacks that "majesty of passion that sweeps the mind from its seat," the passion that is "possessed by nearly every man once in his life" (161). Philip Fisher makes the point that Dreiser's emphasis here is a Darwinian one, namely that such passion belongs only to youth and is connected to the urge for reproduction.[15] Yet it is not only Hurstwood who – "being an older man" (161) – lacks the capacity for such passion. No character in *Sister Carrie* is susceptible to experience of this kind. Indeed, the nearest approach to such feeling may be made by Carrie herself – as Laura.

Carrie's appearance in *Under the Gaslight* is the "once in [her] life" when *she* possesses the "majesty of passion" that imaginatively merges being into otherness, sweeping everything before it.[16] Carrie's closest approach to the desire for "reproduction," however, is the desire for representation – the "outworking of desire to reproduce life" that, according to the narrative voice, is "the basis of all dramatic art" (117).[17]

Within the text of *Sister Carrie* the theatre emerges as an arena for the flow of desire, expressed both in the very act of representation and in the interaction between performer and spectator. But Carrie's "desire to reproduce life," as expressed on stage through her histrionic gift, fulfills a number of other functions that underscore the difference between desire as passion and desire as representation. For one thing, the organization of the theatre enforces that separation between audience and actress that allows Carrie unabashedly to display her desire-full self, without risking its being appropriated.

If Drouet's presence in the wings is one of the indispensable conditions for realization of that "power which to [Hurstwood and Drouet] was a revelation" (140), so at the same time Carrie's freedom to let go and enact the "old melancholy of desire" depends upon the special conditions of the theatre. It is only there, playing the role of another woman, that Carrie can be sure of maintaining the distance between herself and those members of the audience to whom she was "a delicious little morsel . . . [whose] frown they would have loved to force away with kisses" (326). It is true, of course, that the position of the actress involves a kind of selling – or at least renting – of desire and self that has long contributed to the association of actress and prostitute in Western culture.[18] Yet the actress (perhaps like the writer giving autobiographical interviews, or creating fictional self-portraits) also derives a number of benefits from the position of limited exposure. Not the least of these, for Carrie, is the sense of safety and autonomy assured both by the inner "independence of success" that results from her achievement, and by the formalized structure of the theatre itself.[19]

Carrie's most persuasive moments as Laura (both for herself and for the audience) occur when even Carrie is taken in – when she herself merges momentarily with the figure of Laura and no longer knows where she begins and Laura ends. Yet Carrie is not in danger of carrying this merger, this confusion, beyond the limits of the play. By contrast, Drouet and Hurstwood, swooning with love for Carrie, are in a position of much greater risk. Unable to distinguish Carrie from Laura, they are comic as well as pathetic. "[H]e would have that lovely girl if it took his all" (140) Hurstwood thinks to himself (rather prophetically) after watching Carrie play Laura. Indeed, in pursuit of his wish to appropriate Carrie, Hurstwood effectively closes the distance between stage and audience – and lives to regret it.

In the early phases of her relationship with Hurstwood, Carrie is said to be "too full of wonder and desire to be greedy" (91). The implicit polarity between desire and greed here may be curious; but the paradox is typical of Dreiser's rendering of desire throughout *Sister Carrie*. From Dreiser's point of view, while some modes of desire give rise to a feeling of hunger or need that impels the self toward others (and generally leaves it inextricably entangled as a result), certain other modes provide the self with a sense of plenitude that becomes, in turn, a source of power and autonomy.

Desire in *Sister Carrie*, as I have suggested, takes many forms. But the only safe desire – one that revitalizes rather than destroys – is

desire self-sufficient enough to generate its own grounds of satisfaction, self-sufficient enough to enhance rather than undermine
the autonomy of the self. Carrie's respect for autonomy is never
more succinctly expressed than when she voices her admiration
for Robert Ames as the kind of man who "probably could be
happy . . . all alone" (237). Despite Carrie's thirst for the responses
and approval of others, her capacity to endure "alone," if not
necessarily to be "happy," is insured by her histrionic talent, her
own particular brand of self-sustaining desire. "'The world is always struggling to express itself,'" Robert Ames tells Carrie.

> "Most people are not capable of voicing their feelings. They depend
> upon others. That is what genius is for. One man expresses their
> desires for them in music; another one in poetry; another one in a
> play. Sometimes nature does it in a face – it makes the face repre-
> sentative of all desire. That's what has happened in your case."
> (356)

The expressive gift (musical, poetic, or dramatic) seems to expand
the self by allowing it to represent and even merge with otherness,
while simultaneously defending it against the vulnerability such a
merger might imply. Once Carrie finds herself subject to "the flood
of feeling" released by Hurstwood's glance, permeated by that "atmosphere which suffuses her being" (88), she has begun that process of drift which takes her out "into deep water" and allows "her
few supports [to] float away from her" (89).[20] Throughout *Sister
Carrie* this tempting, pleasurable dissolution or abandonment of
self is a component of two related but quite different processes:
erotic passion and the desire for representation. Both kinds of
desire create an atmosphere in which the limits of reality (including the barriers between self and other) seem to fade. If sexual
desire makes the self more vulnerable, more dependent on the
other, however, the desire for representation, as we have seen, has
precisely the opposite effect – for a while.

In one of his more famous formulations, Dreiser speaks of the
critical "balancing stage" (239) after which a man's fortune, his
bodily growth – and capacity for desire – inevitably declines. Walter Benn Michaels notes that Dreiser proposes two possible options
for extending the limited life cycle of desire and fortune: either die
young, and thus "escape the long, slow diminution of desire";[21] or

become enormously wealthy, and thus ally one's fortune "with young forces" (240). "What the rich man buys with his money," in Michaels's account, "is the young man's desire."[22] Similarly, as Fred G. See puts it, "More than anything else, Hurstwood desires [Carrie's] desire."[23]

Access to another person's money, energy, or desire, however, is not to be had for free. Indeed, as Hurstwood learns to his cost, the price of appropriating desire can be fatally high. Within *Sister Carrie,* only the desire for representation affords the self a secure vantage point from which to experience "joys and sorrows which we may never be permitted to feel on our own behalf" (177 Penn). Only on stage (or in her rocking chair) can Carrie experience the full force of the "old melancholy of desire" without courting disaster.

Carrie's ability to represent desire, then, is at once her most precious possession and her most marketable asset, an eminently practical and yet an almost magical resource. For unlike either wealth or the life cycle of energy and desire in Dreiser's paradigm, Carrie's talent is seen to be not only self-sustaining (or self-expanding), but potentially inexhaustible: "Use," as Ames puts it, "will make your powers endure. . . . You will have them so long as they express something in you. You can preserve and increase them longer by using them for others" (485 Penn; cf. 356 N). According to Ames, the capacity for representation – unique in the world of *Sister Carrie* – actually increases with the spending.

Clearly Carrie's histrionic gift, whatever its drawbacks, is to be distinguished not only from the common experience but also from the common objects of desire. As Philip Fisher suggests, "the life history of [an object] is one of continual decline. All goods are used up and replaced."[24] By contrast, Carrie's self-sustaining, revitalizing talent might be more aptly compared to Marx's hoard of capital (which creates value only if spent),[25] or to Walter Benjamin's characterization of narrative itself in his essay "The Storyteller." In an attempt to articulate "the nature of true storytelling" Benjamin differentiates between "information" and "a story." "The value of information," Benjamin writes, "does not survive the moment in which it was new. It lives only at that moment. . . . a story is different. It does not expend itself."[26] Dreiser's rendering of Carrie's mimetic gift has much in common with Benjamin's effort to describe "true storytelling." Not only is Carrie's talent, like Benjamin's story, seen as self-sustaining and potentially inexhaustible but, like the storyteller's tale, Carrie's capacity for representation, to be perpetuated, ultimately depends upon the responsiveness of others.

It is not "use" alone, in Ames's formulation, that will ensure the preservation of Carrie's "powers." Use *for others* is the sine qua non of the representational impulse. If, as Ames says, "the world" needs "genius" in order to "express itself" (356), "genius," by the same token, needs the world. Without Drouet, Hurstwood, and finally Ames to elicit and focus her desire (both for the "other" and for representation itself) Carrie remains essentially passive. Hurstwood's own final passivity is compounded, as well as partially accounted for, not only by his "failure of desire" but by the loss of his own capacity for self-representation, and his progressive retreat from all contact.[27]

By contrast, the life-giving properties of representation are illustrated in the following vignette from Dreiser's description of his dying brother Paul. In one of their final encounters, Paul spoke

> of his early life, the romance of it – maybe I could write a story sometime, tell something about him! . . . To please him I made notes. . . . *On these occasions he was always his old self*, full of ridiculous stories, quips and slight *mots*, all in his old and best vein. *He would soon be himself, he now insisted.*[28] (emphasis supplied)

In this account of Paul, even being oneself is conceived not only as a function of representation (in this case through storytelling) but even as a collaborative effort. It is as if Paul needs the story of his own past reflected back to him through the prospect of his brother's writing in order to "be himself." Such being, moreover, is no sooner said than done: Already, as Dreiser notes, "on these occasions he was always his old self," producing stories of his own.

As Dreiser sees it, representation implicitly facilitates not only human interaction but "being" as such. Conversely, reciprocity – sustained interaction with others – would appear to be almost indispensable to the act of representation, whether in narrative, in the theatre, or in some other form. Dreiser's rendering of his songwriter–brother repeatedly confirms his sense of the artist's need for contact with others in the course of creative activity. Using language that recalls Drouet's support for Carrie in *Under the Gaslight*, Dreiser describes Paul's own lifelong need for "someone to buoy him up, a manager, a strong confidant of some kind" (268).[29] According to Dreiser, Paul was never as happy as during the process of composition itself, an activity that tended to begin with improvisation, but which at a certain stage (like Carrie's first performance and Dreiser's own work) invariably involved the participation of someone else. Dreiser reports Paul's repeatedly calling him over to the piano ("[l]isten to this will you, Thee?") only to stop himself shortly with tears in his eyes, too moved to go on (261–2).[30]

We have seen that a responsive audience enhances the pleasures of representation – whether on stage, on a carriage ride, or in a rocking chair. Moreover, even as Ames appreciates Carrie's ability to express "the world's longings," it would appear that he himself serves an analogous function for her. While he talks of happiness and failure, Balzac and desire, Carrie watches him "closely. . . . He seemed to be stating her case" (482 Penn). Just as she expresses his feelings and desires, he expresses hers.

Representation, moreover, is seen to be not only a reciprocal but also an intimate process. When Carrie plays Laura at Avery Hall, Hurstwood – like others in the audience – "could almost feel that she was talking to him. . . . Pathos has this quality, that it seems ever addressed to one alone" (137). If a sense of intimacy and reciprocity may attend the realization of Carrie's powers at their best, however, these qualities are particularly scarce amid the characteristic anonymity, publicity, and fragmentation of Dreiser's Chicago and New York.

Walter Benjamin's reflections in "The Storyteller" thus have a further relevance to the issues under consideration here.[31] I have already suggested that Carrie's ultimate isolation may reflect Dreiser's fears or ambivalence about his own professional ambitions. Benjamin's analysis of the isolation that afflicts the modern novelist may help to explain why Dreiser uses the figure of Carrie the actress as a stand-in for the figure of the writer, underscoring both similarities and differences between the actress and the novelist. I have been stressing the analogies between Carrie and Dreiser not only in terms of the governing impulses and inherent rewards of imaginative representation, but also in terms of the actress/writer's need for encouraging feedback and moral support. We have seen that Carrie's final distance from her audience – "her lonely, self-withdrawing temper" (353) which itself serves to make her "an interesting figure in the public eye" (353) – provides a stark contrast to her first acting experience. But it simultaneously provides a resonant image for what we might take to be Dreiser's own position as an American writer at the turn of the century.

Benjamin's discussion of the isolated modern novelist takes as its point of reference, or point of contrast, the lost art of oral storytelling. For Benjamin, the storyteller's contact with his audience not only kept narrative within the "realm of living speech" (87), it also encouraged (and depended on) "the gift for listening" and "the community of listeners" (91). In Benjamin's account, moreover, the isolation of the novelist is mirrored by that of the reader: "A man listening to a story is in the company of the story-teller; even a man reading one shares this companionship. The reader of a novel, however, is isolated, more so than any other reader."[32] Thus the rewards of oral storytelling, from Benjamin's point of view, are antithetical to the work of the professional novelist. Yet Benjamin's somewhat nostalgic sense of what has been lost, reproduces, in another form, Dreiser's own fascination with modes of representation and performance that, unlike writing, may be readily perceived in terms of human interaction, and even eros.

In a sense, Dreiser's process of composition, especially his involvement with others throughout, partially restored the rewards of the oral storyteller to the work of the latter-day novelist. Dreiser may well have hoped for commensurate satisfactions after publication of the novel. According to Swanberg, Dreiser felt he had written "a great book which the public could not fail to recognize";[33] but his keenest rewards in writing *Sister Carrie* may have ended with his completion of the manuscript.

By conceiving of Carrie's talent as a quality that (like Walter Benjamin's story) "does not expend itself," Dreiser endows Carrie's representational gift with properties that at once epitomize and appear to transcend the prevailing cultural norms of value and success. When Carrie, in the process of representation, experiences that joyful sense of autonomy and plenitude that renders other people momentarily superfluous, she achieves a brief escape from the power struggles and market relationships that seem to color all human contacts in a world where everything has a price.

Yet if Carrie on stage at the Avery Theatre – perhaps like Dreiser himself in the act of composition – comes to experience her deepest feelings and greatest satisfactions, there are pitfalls just the same, both in collaborative interaction with others and in the exhilarating sense of autonomy that follows. These pitfalls appear well before individual members of the audience bid for possession of the actress, and well before autonomy turns into isolation. As soon as the "independence of success" begins to stir in Carrie's heart and she begins to move "out of the ranks of the suppliants into the lines of the dispensers of charity" (144), the vocabulary of power, social standing, and economics that governs her experience off stage is already reasserting its priority. It is perhaps in this sense that Carrie is indeed "as happy as ever she would be" when her desire for imaginative representation is fulfilled in the solitude of her rocking chair, rather than in public.

The end of *Sister Carrie* returns Carrie to her rocking chair once more – but now she herself is a reader of novels. As Donald Pizer points out, the irony implicit in Carrie's sympathetic response to *Père Goriot* (while Hurstwood dies, unnoticed) is analogous to the irony of Carrie's success in playing the virtuous Laura.[34] But this irony may also provide a sardonic comment on the limitations of "sympathetic" readers. While Dreiser may have wished *Sister Carrie* readers as appreciative as Arthur Henry or Frank Norris,[35] he may already have suspected, as he wrote the novel's final scenes, that he would have, at best, readers with the imperfect understanding, if ready sympathy, of Carrie herself reading Balzac.

Dreiser seems to have experienced the lack of response to his first published novel as his worst nightmare come true. In the absence of the saving, revitalizing feedback he must have craved, it is hardly surprising that he felt he could no longer write. Once he began to recover from the ensuing emotional and financial crisis – but before devoting himself fully to the work of a second novel – Dreiser diverted his substantial energies into a brief but highly successful career editing popular women's magazines. The nature of that success provides a comic footnote to his lifelong bid for the receptive attention of an audience. Following what Swanberg calls his "sudden hunches about reader interest," Dreiser launched a variety of contests and columns that elicited unprecedented reader response. He "wheedled women readers into regarding the Butterick magazines as their friend and tutor," Swanberg writes, "so that more than 9,000 readers' letters a month came into the beauty department alone."[36] Perhaps the steadily rising circulation at Butterick's provided some compensation for the grim silence Dreiser felt had greeted *Sister Carrie*.

"Narrative," as Peter Brooks puts it, "implies narrating." But since, as Brooks notes, "the modern writer will never experience . . . the communicative situation" that the oral storyteller takes for granted,[37] the twentieth-century novelist must aim at other satisfactions. It is particularly fitting that the young Dreiser should have dreamed not only of writing for the stage,[38] but even of being "a great orator" speaking to "thousands of . . . hearers moved to tears or demonstrations of wild delight."[39] By the time Dreiser wrote *Sister Carrie*, of course, his wish to stand before an audience in person had apparently been replaced by a wish to appear in print. As I have tried to show, however, Dreiser's rendering of Carrie's histrionic process suggests that he continued to covet an ongoing relationship with some kind of responsive audience. Indeed, his rendering of Carrie (like his rendering of Paul) and his own habits of composition would all seem to reflect Dreiser's conviction that, as Robert Ames tells Carrie, "only use . . . for others" can make the artist's "powers endure."

NOTES

1. The most notorious such account is Dreiser's version of how *Sister Carrie*, originally accepted for publication, was later rejected and "suppressed" because of the moral outrage of Mrs. Doubleday. For a recent analysis of this episode see Stephen C. Brennan, "The Publication of *Sister Carrie*: Old and New Fictions," *American Literary Realism* 18 (1985): 55; see also W. A. Swanberg, *Dreiser* (New York: Scribners, 1965), pp. 85–8, 92–3, 128.

2. Quoted by Dorothy Dudley, *Forgotten Frontiers: Dreiser and the Land of the Free* (New York: Smith and Haas, 1932), p. 160. Donald Pizer points out that Dreiser confirmed the story again years later. See *The Novels of Theodore Dreiser* (Minneapolis: University of Minnesota Press, 1976), pp. 43, 352 n20.

3. Dreiser's full description is cited in Pizer, *Novels*, p. 46.

4. See Donald Pizer, "Self-Censorship and Textual Editing," in *Textual Criticism and Literary Interpretation*, ed. Jerome J. McGann (Chicago: University of Chicago Press, 1985), p. 157; "*Sister Carrie*: Manuscript to Print," in James L. W. West III et. al., eds., *Sister Carrie: The Pennsylvania Edition* (Philadelphia: University of Pennsylvania Press, 1981), pp. 503–19; Stephen C. Brennan, "The Composition of *Sister Carrie*: A Reconsideration," *Dreiser Newsletter* 9 (Fall 1978): 17–23; and Swanberg, *Dreiser*, pp. 83–5.

5. Among the most heavily reworked portions of the manuscript is its conclusion. Dreiser's "inspiration" notwithstanding, the holograph contains thirteen pages of notes by Henry and by Dreiser's wife, Jug, about the ending of the book. See West, "Manuscript to Print," p. 516; see also Pizer, *Novels*, pp. 46, 352 n26.

6. Cited in Ellen Moers, *Two Dreisers* (New York: Viking, 1969), pp. 115–17; Swanberg, *Dreiser*, p. 54.

7. On the unprecedented concern with the author as a commodity see Daniel H. Borus, *Writing Realism: Howells, James and Norris in the Mass Market* (Chapel Hill: University of North Carolina Press, 1989). Borus suggests that, at the turn of the century, the public became as interested in consuming the writer as in consuming the books that the writer produced, and that writers assiduously contributed to their own packaging.

8. In an early piece entitled "The Return of Genius," Dreiser depicts the repeated intervention of the "God of Genius" on behalf of a young man who longs for fame and fortune. In another early essay Dreiser argues outright that America needs a system of patronage for genius. See *Theodore Dreiser: A Selection of Uncollected Prose*, ed. Donald Pizer (Detroit: Wayne State University Press, 1977), pp. 33–5, 36–8; see also "The Real Howells," *Uncollected Prose*, pp. 141–6.

9. Unless otherwise indicated, all references are to the Norton Critical Edition of *Sister Carrie*. References to the Pennsylvania Edition are indicated by "Penn" following the page number.

10. The moral contrast between Carrie and Laura is the source of the scene's well-known irony; see Philip Fisher, *Hard Facts* (New York: Oxford University Press, 1985), p. 166; Moers, *Two Dreisers*, pp. 110–

11; Pizer, *Novels*, p. 94. Yet Carrie does have fleeting moments of regret over the virtuous maiden she might have been.

11. On the importance of watching and being watched as a trope within American realism see Mark Seltzer, "Physical Capital: *The American* and the Realist Body," in *New Essays on The American*, ed. Martha Banta (Cambridge University Press, 1987), p. 134 and "*The Princess Casamassima:* Realism and the Fantasy of Surveillance," in Eric Sundquist, ed., *American Realism: New Essays* (Baltimore: Johns Hopkins University Press, 1982), p. 112; see also Fisher, *Hard Facts*, pp. 156–7.

12. Carrie's performance at Avery Hall has long been the focus of critical comment. See Pizer's discussion of the structural problem created by this premature climax of Carrie's career (*Novels*, pp. 69, 83; cf. pp. 41–2, 94); see also Deborah M. Garfield, "Taking a Part: Actor and Audience in Theodore Dreiser's *Sister Carrie*," *American Literary Realism* 16 (1983): 232–4; Moers, *Two Dreisers*, pp. 109–11; Hugh Witemeyer, "Gaslight and Magic Lamp in *Sister Carrie*," *PMLA* 86 (1971): 230–40.

13. Richard Poirier, "Panoramic Environment and the Anonymity of the Self," in the Norton Critical Edition of *Sister Carrie*, p. 580.

14. The same process is repeated in Carrie's best scene – she becomes impervious to "the acting of others" (139); cf. the first rehearsal (125).

15. Fisher, *Hard Facts*, p. 172.

16. Compare Pizer's consideration of Carrie's waning sexuality, *Novels*, pp. 71–2. See also Fred G. See, "The Text as Mirror: *Sister Carrie* and the Lost Language of the Heart," *Criticism* 20 (1978): 159; and Walter Benn Michaels, "Sister Carrie's Popular Economy," *Critical Inquiry* 7 (Winter 1980): 385, 387.

17. Compare Michaels, "Popular Economy," pp. 383–4, and Seltzer on "forms of reproduction" in *The American* in his "Physical Capital," pp. 135–8.

18. See Fisher, *Hard Facts*, pp. 134, 167, 174; and Janet Blair, "Private Parts in Public Places: The Case of Actresses," in *Women in Space: Ground Rules and Social Maps*, ed. Shirley Ardener (New York: St. Martin's, 1981), pp. 211, 215, 219.

19. See Blair, "Private Parts," pp. 212, 216; Fisher, *Hard Facts*, p. 166.

20. Dreiser's rendering of Carrie's attraction to Hurstwood consistently suggests a sense of suffusion and dissolution which neutralizes the autonomous activity of the self. Compare Hurstwood's "permeating grace" (102); "the atmosphere which [he] created for her" (148); "the glow of his temperament, and the light of his eye [that she could

not resist]" (149). When Hurstwood's eyes flash "a subtle dissolving fire" Carrie is "overwhelmed" (150).

21. Michaels, "Popular Economy," p. 387.

22. Ibid.

23. See "Text as Mirror," p. 156; compare Fisher's analysis of this passage in *Hard Facts*, pp. 173–4.

24. Fisher, *Hard Facts*, p. 175.

25. Compare Michaels, "Popular Economy," p. 386.

26. Walter Benjamin, "The Storyteller," in *Illuminations*, trans. Harry Zohn (New York: Schocken Books, 1969), p. 90. With Benjamin's formulation in mind, *Sister Carrie* may be seen as a kind of rewriting of Balzac's *The Wild Ass's Skin* – one of Dreiser's favorite novels, and a touchstone in recent discussions of narrative theory. (See Leo Bersani, *A Future for Astyanax* [Boston: Little Brown, 1976], pp. 70–4; Peter Brooks, *Reading for the Plot* [New York: Knopf, 1984]; and compare Michaels, "Popular Economy," pp. 385–7.) In Balzac's tale, Raphael's life span is shortened every time he uses the magical skin to facilitate fulfillment of desire. But unlike Raphael's desire, unlike Dreiser's paradigm of fortune and bodily growth, and unlike the "life" of commodities in the world of *Sister Carrie*, Carrie's histrionic talent, fueled by desire, is an infinitely expanding asset that renews itself, rather than consumes itself, with use. Compare See, "Text as Mirror," p. 156.

27. See Michaels, "Popular Economy," p. 386 and compare his "Introduction" to *The Gold Standard and the Logic of Naturalism* (Berkeley: University of California Press, 1987), p. 19.

28. Theodore Dreiser, "My Brother Paul," in *The Best Short Stories of Theodore Dreiser* (Cleveland: World, 1941), p. 269. Further references to this essay will be included in the text.

29. This description contains striking echoes of Carrie's appearance as Laura, not only because Drouet "buoys [Carrie] up" in the wings, but also because Hurstwood ("the manager"!) secures a friendly, well-disposed audience for the show.

30. On Paul's role in Dreiser's career as a writer, see Moers, *Two Dreisers*, pp. 85–9, 94–8; see also Philip Gerber, "A Star is Born: Celebrity in *Sister Carrie*," *Dreiser Studies* 19 (1988): 9–11.

31. For a pertinent analysis of Benjamin's essay, see Peter Brooks, "The Tale vs. the Novel," *Novel* 21 (Winter/Spring 1988): 285–92.

32. Benjamin, "The Storyteller," p. 100.

33. Swanberg, *Dreiser*, p. 90.

34. Pizer, *Novels*, pp. 71, 94.

35. Norris was the reader at Doubleday who enthusiastically accepted Dreiser's manuscript for publication.
36. Swanberg, *Dreiser*, pp. 128–9.
37. Brooks, "Tale vs. Novel," p. 286.
38. "My bent, if you will believe it, was plays," Dreiser wrote to Mencken in 1916. (Robert Elias, ed., *Letters of Theodore Dreiser* [Philadelphia: University of Pennsylvania Press, 1959], vol. 1, p. 213.) See Dreiser, *A Book About Myself* (New York: Boni and Liveright, 1922), pp. 173–80, on his work as drama critic for the St. Louis *Globe-Democrat*, and his own aspirations as a playwright; see also Moers, *Two Dreisers*, pp. 75, 330 n 5; and Swanberg, *Dreiser*, pp. 44–5.
39. Theodore Dreiser, *A Book About Myself*, p. 3.

4

Sister Carrie: The City, the Self, and the Modes of Narrative Discourse

RICHARD LEHAN

1

W E NOW know that the summer of 1894 was an intellectual turning point for Theodore Dreiser. At that time, as a reporter for the Pittsburgh *Dispatch,* he would spend his free time in the public library reading Herbert Spencer and Honoré de Balzac. The experience, he has told us, "quite blew me, intellectually, to bits."[1]

It is hard to imagine Dreiser, with only a semester of college and no formal training in philosophy, reading Spencer in any sophisticated way. But when one looks at the uses that Dreiser made of Spencer – first in his philosophical essays as "The Prophet," and later in *Sister Carrie* – one must modify this conclusion. Spencer's philosophy is a nineteenth-century combination of mechanistic and romantic belief. Like the mechanistic Thomas Hobbes, Spencer believed that we live in a world composed of matter in motion: such matter makes up the natural process, which is both repeatable and hence describable in scientific terms. Like the romantics, Spencer also believed that nature symbolically reflected its inner meaning, so that to read the universe was to read the unfolding of nature and to understand the correspondences that existed between man and (say) the animal world.

The key to Spencer's philosophy was his belief in force – not a life force as in Bergson, where the impetus comes from within, but a force that manifested itself from without. Force itself is a constant (what Spencer called the "persistence of force"). One force, however, generates its opposite: "there cannot be an isolated force beginning and ending in nothing; . . . any force . . . implies an equal antecedent force from which it is derived, and against which

65

it is a reaction."[2] We lift a stone through the force of our muscles, but the weight of the stone and the force of gravity create a counterforce, which in turn sets limits to what we can lift. So in life: we are surrounded by physical forces that set limits to our mental expectations and to our ability for unrestrained action. As we become more powerful agents of force ourselves, we can widen those limits, move beyond previous physical restraints – up to a point. We then reach a realm beyond which we cannot go – what Spencer awkwardly called the point of "equilibration," and Dreiser the "equation inevitable." This point of stasis brings on a reversal in the flow of matter, and a process of dissolution takes over. Thus, while the fate of the individual is cyclical (a process of birth and growth that leads toward development and maturity, followed eventually by physical and mental decline, and ultimately death), the fate of the race is onward and upward.

The idea of cycles within the march of time was central to Spencer's belief in the progress of evolution, the idea that mankind was advancing even while the fate of the individual was circumscribed within physical limits. Spencer believed that all matter was thus passing from homogeneity to heterogeneity – that is, from the more simple toward the more complex, at which point an equilibrium occurs, followed by dissolution and new forms of homogeneity, as the cycle repeats itself.

For Spencer the primary force in the universe is the sun. The sun's heat and light is the source of all life, and thus the mover of all movers. The cooling of the great heavenly bodies allowed the material systems of the universe to come into being; these systems are more complex (heterogeneous) than the gases out of which they originated. Society itself is an organic unit subject to undirected physical or manmade forces (FP, 226). Spencer believed that historically mankind was moving away from slave and military societies, characterized by uniformity (homogeneity), toward industrial societies characterized by skills (heterogeneity) and specializations. Even though we create gigantic cities, we can never escape our essential relationship to nature. We are all affected by such primary events as harvests and droughts: a bad wheat crop affects every member of a society. As in nature, the fittest will survive (a Spencerian idea often attributed to Darwin). Spencer was not a man of sentiment: it was the law of nature that creatures not energetic enough to sustain themselves must die.

Spencer's *First Principles* can serve as a key to Dreiser's *Sister Carrie*. Dreiser's first novel is an exercise in the principle of matter in motion – moving toward a completion in Carrie, a form of stasis or equilibrium in Drouet, and a process of dissolution in Hurstwood. The main force at work in the novel is that of the city, seen first in a less complex form embodied by Chicago, and then in a more complex (heterogeneous) form embodied by New York. Dreiser describes the city most vividly at night, when its lights suggest a kind of inner energy like the light of the sun. The city is repeatedly described as a magnet, a compelling attraction, drawing people to it with pulsating energy. Urban crowds are matter in motion, sweeping onward, like the sea, through space and time. In fact, Dreiser tells us that the pull of the sun and the moon creates the tides of the sea, the rhythm of which is embodied in the city, in the flux of the crowd, and in Carrie and later Hurstwood rocking in their rocking chairs.

All of the characters in the novel are caught within the circumference of this materiality: while Carrie is able to enlarge her circumference of being, Hurstwood's gets smaller and smaller, leaving him little operating room and finally no choice. The self is thus defined from without – that is, externally – within the realm of such materiality: take away Drouet's clothes and, Dreiser tells us, "he was nothing"; take away Hurstwood's managerial position and he becomes nothing;[3] and take away Carrie's connection to the theater and she too becomes devoid of self. Unlike the novels of comic realism, *Sister Carrie* has no moral center – no Squire Allworthy, or Mr. Knightley, or Joe Gargery, or Esther Summerson through which to center moral truth. What we get is human experience as an amoral process; characters moved around like driftwood caught in the ocean's tide, never able to contextualize their place in the process, always being spoken through by a larger self, which is the voice of the city itself, and by the desire its materiality produces.

Free will is negated because all choice is weighted: Carrie's decision to live with Drouet, Hurstwood's decision to steal the money, Carrie's decision to accompany Hurstwood to Montreal and then to New York, Carrie's decision to leave Hurstwood, and Hurstwood's decision to commit suicide – all are weighted choices, by which I mean there is more weight (force) on one side of the equation than on the other; the decision is thus always predetermined, the compulsion and pull in one direction much greater than the resistance in the other – as we see when Hurstwood tells himself that stealing the money from the safe will lead only to futility, and yet he has no power to resist. As the heliotrope turns toward the sun, all of Dreiser's characters turn to the lights of the city, and then within the city are moved by its materiality to objects of desire that they cannot resist. The sun heats the land, creates the convectionary winds that turn to clouds, the clouds to vapor, the vapor to rain, the rain to irrigated land, the land to harvested crops, and the crops to sustained life, so the city creates its own energy, out of which come the institutions (the sweatshops in which Carrie first works) which bring forth material goods (the clothes and the trinkets) and the social play (life in the theater, the hotels, the restaurants) that she finds so compelling. And just as the planets cannot go beyond the limits set by the solar system, so Dreiser's characters cannot go beyond the limits set by money. Unlike a novel by Henry James, where money is seldom discussed, Dreiser's novel accounts for each penny that comes to its main characters, and Carrie's rise and Hurstwood's fall are both measured in terms of their rising and falling incomes. Thus, like Spencer's, Dreiser's world is one of physical limits – a world in which the self constantly tests such limits, held in a process of expansion and contraction, and thus establishes the physical realm beyond which the individual, the crowd, the city, and even the earth itself cannot go.

2

Dreiser begins his novel with Carrie Meeber coming to Chicago from Columbia City (Green Bay, Wisconsin, in the holograph) on the train, where she meets Drouet. By the middle of the novel, Carrie is on another train with Hurstwood, who is taking her to Montreal and later to New York. At the very end of the novel, Mrs. Hurstwood and her family also come into New York on a train.

Trains bring all of the major characters either into or out of the city – and Dreiser's novel plays itself out against the meaning and values of the urban world. Near the end of the novel, Robert Ames tells Carrie to read Balzac, and one of the last sights we have is of her reading *Père Goriot*. Ames also recommends Balzac's *The Great Man from the Provinces* sequence – an appropriate choice, it would seem, since Dreiser's own novel is also working in the same sub-genre, using the young man from the provinces formula closely associated with Balzac, but also practiced by other nineteenth-century novelists, such as Dickens in *Great Expectations*.

The young man from the provinces subgenre involves a predictable sequence of events. First we have the sense that the provinces or the estate is played out – that the city is where the young must go in order to realize a heightened sense of self, a kind of essential being. This in turn brings a break with the family, whose residual values the hero takes to the city, where they must ultimately be abandoned. The reality of love and friendship does not prove very substantial in the city, where almost everything turns on money and where personal relationships are inseparable from commodity relationships. The city itself is so much larger than the individual that the human scale is lost – as well as the values that go with the human scale – and the hero spends much of the novel simply trying to reinvest energy in a system that proves to be both a compelling lure and a trap. Such novels often address the need to find an alternate set of human values; but attempts to redeem the city usually are unsuccessful, and the main character is left confronting the same world, only now a bit disillusioned, as well as a bit more experienced and a lot more wary.

Dreiser makes use of this narrative pattern, but in the naturalistic mode rather than in the mode of comic realism of Balzac or Dickens. As a result, there are radical differences between a novel like *Sister Carrie* and Balzac's *Lost Illusions*. First, Dreiser spends very little time dealing with the reasons Carrie leaves her family to go to the city. The novel simply assumes that the city is where someone with her disposition and temperament would go. There is hardly a reference to Carrie's mother in any draft of the novel, and the father appears only as a memory as her train passes the flour plant in which he works as a laborer. Carrie, of course, will live with her sister and her sister's husband in Chicago, so the novel does not really begin with a clean break from the family. But the Hansons are such dour people that Carrie soon understands that she cannot realize the kind of life she has dreamed about with them. Hanson, the son of immigrants, cleans refrigerator cars in a railroad compound connected to the stockyards. Carrie's sister gets up every morning at 4:40; Hanson rises soon after, and does not return from work until after seven in the evening. Despite his small earnings, he is paying on two lots of land in the West End on which he plans to build. One may assume that someday he will be comfortably situated, but for the moment his only worldly pleasures involve a pair of yellow slippers, and daily play before dinner with his infant son. Like her husband, Carrie's sister is defined mainly by a sense of duty and an almost nonexistent sense of pleasure. Carrie has no desire to defer pleasure in such a way, and she will reverse the Hansons' formula of success.

It does not take Carrie long to discover that almost every relationship she incurs is involved with money. She quickly realizes that the Hansons have invited her to live with them because they expect to use the bulk of her pay for their household expenses and to increase payments on the land they have bought. Carrie's initial experience in the city involves a job in a shoe factory, where she operates a machine on an assembly line from eight until six o'clock, with a half hour for lunch, for $4.50 a week – a little over seventy cents a day. (Carrie would now be working for less than thirty dollars a day.) Given the weight that money has in her world, the offer of twenty dollars from Drouet involves an immense amount (the equivalent of about $800 today, or over a month's salary). To speak in such terms about character relationships catches both the spirit and the method of Dreiser's technique: almost everything is quantified, and usually quantified in monetary terms. It is not accidental, for example, that when Carrie leaves Hurstwood, she will also leave him twenty dollars, the same sum that Drouet gave to her. In this novel everything, including love and friendship, has a price.

Different also from the traditional young man from the provinces, Carrie does not have any full-blown sense of what she wants to be. We assume that she has left the small town out of

70

boredom and has only the vaguest idea of what she might become in the city. And yet the city does indeed reveal to her an inner self – capabilities she was not aware of back in Columbia City and which she discovers only when she goes on the stage as an amateur actress in Chicago. All kinds of mysteries lie buried in the city, including the mystery of the inner self. Carrie seems to intuit this from the beginning. She senses even from the train the energy of the city, feels its flow embodied in the crowds that she watches from Hanson's doorstep, as well as in the public space (avenues, parks, restaurants, hotels) that immediately catch her attention. And indeed the connection between the stage and the city is a real one. When Drouet takes her into a restaurant to buy a sumptuous meal, they sit beside a window and watch the city flow by as if on a stage. Hurstwood will repeat this scene at the end of the novel when he looks out the window of a New York hotel at a panorama of the city.

Walter Benjamin tells us that the flaneur goes to the city to observe. But in so doing, the flaneur is also observed: the spectator becomes spectacle. Benjamin also tells us that Baudelaire went to the crowd in order to be alone, by which he meant in order to lose his individual self in the tide of humanity, to gain a kind of release in the power of anonymity.[4] Carrie shares such feelings. She takes her being from the city's energy, intuits its material nature, intuits that its very flow is inseparable from the crowds that embody it. So to be a part of the crowd is to be a part of an urban process, part of its spectacle – to both observe and be observed in this play (that is, this drama) of life. When Carrie walks down Broadway, she feels that she is part of a larger theater. "Such feelings as were generated in Carrie by this walk," we are told, "put her in an exceedingly receptive mood for the pathos which followed in the play" (227). When Hurstwood is pulled from the streetcar by the angry mob of strikers, he feels himself drawn into an energy that is like a roiling sea, the metaphor Dreiser most often uses to suggest the ebb and flow of the city's movements. When Carrie succeeds on the stage, she does more than conquer Broadway; she conquers the city itself, of which Broadway is the metonymic equivalent.

That there is more to know about the city, that there are higher planes of artistic reality than the Broadway stage – these are the lessons toward which Ames points Carrie. Ames's function in the novel is indeed to humanize the city in the same way that detectives like Inspector Bucket or Inspector Heat humanize the city in Dickens or Conrad. In an earlier draft of the novel, Ames calls Carrie's attention to the conspicuous consumption at Sherry's and points her toward more serious ways of thinking about her life and surroundings. If the city instills desire, Carrie will be subject to desire so long as she is part of her environment. As the coda of the novel clearly tells us, such desire will never be satisfied; the whole logic of the city is to excite and stimulate, to postulate a simultaneous realm of compelling possibilities. But Ames adds to this the element of discernment, the matter of taste. It is interesting that Dreiser's city is most often characterized by its lights, which illuminate the night; and it is Ames, the electrical engineer, who has invented a new kind of electric light, a new mode of illumination. There is, of course, a double meaning here: just as Ames adds to the city lights, he illuminates Carrie and gives her the means to see. When Hurstwood commits suicide, he does so at night, in a room without a window, where he gives himself to the "kindness" of the night, the energy drained from him and not replenished. The night here embodies the other side of the city's energy, that motion that has taken Hurstwood full cycle back toward dissolution and decay. Like a cold, dead satellite, Hurstwood is no longer capable of being warmed by the urban sun.

Dreiser's city is thus a larger stage. Carrie is brought into a new kind of self when she plays the part of Laura in Augustin Daly's *Under the Gaslight*. Carrie is effective in this role because she can identify with Laura, can feel the social injustice that becomes Laura's fate. When she went to live with Drouet, Carrie experienced similar feelings – the feelings of an outcast. Dreiser sets up physical equivalents in the novel that give substance to the drama of life and art. Because human experience unfolds within a material circumference, we get the repetitive movement that is the staple of Dreiser's narrative method. The reality of one scene becomes the motive for the next: Hurstwood's pull between duty and desire repeats the tug of motives Carrie experiences when she takes Drouet's money, and anticipates the internal struggle she will have when she decides to accompany Hurstwood to Montreal and New

York. The function of Mrs. Hale, who helps turn Chicago into a realm of desire for Carrie, is repeated in Mrs. Vance in New York. Each plateau Carrie climbs has its own physical limits which she soon exhausts, starting the desiring machine all over again. Her hardship with the Hansons is relieved by the comfort Drouet can give her. Her discontent with the uncouth Drouet is relieved by the more sophisticated and caring manner of Hurstwood, who also reveals a world of finer taste. And the physical world that Hurstwood opens up is supplemented by the intellectual realm toward which Ames points her.

What we have here is Spencerian matter in motion, moving toward more complete forms of fulfillment (that is, from the homogeneous to the heterogeneous). This involves pure mechanistic process. We have a progressive sequence at work here, and the narrative meaning of the novel cannot be divorced from the causality of which it is a part. Reverse any one scene in *Sister Carrie* and the action stops. If Carrie had met Hurstwood, not Drouet, on the train from Wisconsin there would have been no story. At that moment, Hurstwood would have found Carrie too far beneath him. If Carrie had not lived with the Hansons, she would not have been desperate enough to become Drouet's mistress. Without his desire for Carrie, Hurstwood would not have been tempted by the money in the open safe; and Carrie would not have gone to New York with Hurstwood if she had not at that moment exhausted her life with Drouet. The examples could be multiplied. What is important is that these scenes run together like a river running from its source. And like Spencer's evolutionary cycles, Dreiser's river really runs in a circle – from birth to death. Carrie's rise is thus inseparable from Hurstwood's fall. The surroundings that energize her toward new forms of life are the same surroundings that coax Hurstwood into passivity and the decline that leads toward death.

Neither Carrie nor Hurstwood is conscious of the process of which they are a part. Dreiser uses a narrative voice in telling his story that clues the reader into the more philosophical meaning of his story. At one point this voice tells us that the characters in the novel are in a kind of evolutionary halfway house: they are no longer the pure product of animal intuition, but they also do not have anything like fully developed reason. What makes Carrie such a vital character is the keenness of her intuition, the deep feeling that moves her toward a kind of understanding and the empathy she brings both to stage and to life. Dreiser is clearly working here within the naturalistic mode of narrative discourse, using characters that are inseparable from the evolutionary process, subject to the forces of their environment, and at best only dimly aware of the gestalt that holds this process together. We thus do not have the moral center – that realm around which the plot can be recuperated – that characterizes comic realism. And we do not have the kind of unmade world confronted by the pure forms of consciousness that characterizes so much of literary modernism, whether it be the *amor fati* consciousness of Friedrich Nietzsche and Ernest Hemingway, the Bergsonian consciousness of Virginia Woolf and D. H. Lawrence, or the struggling moral consciousness of Henry James and Joseph Conrad. Nor do we have forms of consciousness collapsed into the world of which they are a part – whether into structure, paradigm, or forms of discourse – that characterizes postmodernism. Like Zola's world, Dreiser's narrative is controlled by an observer – not the scientific observer of the experimental novel, nor the whimsical, cosmic observer of Hardy, but more the philosophical observer – a kind of Herbert Spencer telling a Balzacian story about life in urban America near the end of the nineteenth century. Dreiser never really outgrew the influence of Spencer and Balzac on his thinking, and there was no need for him to outgrow the narrative mode they helped him to develop. It was a mode that he found personally convincing, one that accommodated his own artistic temperament – in short, a narrative mode that served him well.

3

I have not meant to suggest by this discussion that literary naturalism is a single monolithic construct. One finds diversity within the realm of naturalism, and one could write a different kind of essay contrasting Dreiser's naturalism with that of Émile Zola or Frank Norris. But while narrative modes are seldom pure, what is often the source of great critical confusion is the bringing to bear of a mode different from naturalism upon the reading of a novel like

Sister Carrie. The history of such misreadings could be the subject of a book in itself; what I propose here – to look at some representative examples of this practice – is much more modest.

I begin with Lionel Trilling, not to disturb a long closed grave, but to address a critical problem inseparable from my reading of *Sister Carrie* – namely, what do we make of the "reality" of Dreiser's texts. In his famous essay "Reality in America," Trilling begins with an attack on Vernon Parrington, who expressed "the chronic American belief that there exists an opposition between reality and mind and that one must enlist oneself in the part of reality."[5] Trilling is annoyed that liberal critics like Parrington were more willing to forgive Dreiser his faults than they were Henry James, because Dreiser was obviously on the side of the poor. "No liberal critic," Trilling continues, "asks the question of Dreiser whether *his* moral preoccupations are going to be useful in confronting the disasters that confront us." Trilling is also annoyed that Dreiser is more easily forgiven because the reality of his fiction seems to be more American than James's expatriated views: "Dreiser is to be accepted and forgiven because his faults are the sad, lovable, honorable faults of reality itself, or of America itself – huge, inchoate, struggling toward expression, caught between the dream of raw power and the dream of morality." One can agree with Trilling up to a point. He is addressing an important problem when he questions the notion of a kind of ideal "reality" from which, he argues, someone like Parrington begins his literary study. But Trilling does not question the idea that we can set up a hierarchy of literary reality; what he wants to do is to substitute James's esthetic "reality" for Dreiser's naturalistic one. That is to say, Trilling distinguishes between the narrative modes of Jamesian modernism and Dreiserian naturalism in order to assert that the former is superior to the latter.

What I find most troubling about Trilling's argument – and it is an argument fairly typical of modernistic criticism – is the notion that there is an essential reality against which a novel can be examined. We seldom see that argument today, because the bulk of postmodern theory has convincingly shown that any reading of a text against a notion of what is properly "real" is both arbitrary and privileged. All we can say today is that the reality of Dreiser's novel is very different from the reality of James's; the critic no longer speaks from a godlike position that allows the authority of preference. That does not mean, however, that we cannot compare and contrast the meanings of texts in different narrative modes.

A look at a naturalistic novel like *Sister Carrie* and a novel of comic realism like *A Modern Instance* (1881) reveals immediately how different narrative modes actually work. Howells's Bartley Hubbard is an ambitious and amoral product of a small Maine town who marries the daughter of the local squire (against the squire's wishes) and comes to Boston to make his fortune in journalism. Like Carrie, he struggles in the indifferent city and subordinates moral scruples to his desires for success and money. But whereas Dreiser looked at Carrie's struggles sympathetically, Howells has nothing but contempt for Bartley. When Bartley absconds to Chicago with $1,200, he has a change of heart by the time he gets to Cleveland. When he comes to buy his return ticket to Boston, however, he discovers that his wallet – with the $1,200 – has been stolen. At this point Howells tells us: "Now he could not return; nothing remained for him but the ruin he had chosen." But, of course, Bartley has not chosen at all – or rather, he has chosen to return to Boston, just the opposite of what fate has allowed. His situation is thus similar to Hurstwood's in *Sister Carrie*: Bartley is driven toward a predestined end by an accident (the stolen wallet) just as Hurstwood is driven toward a predestined end by another accident (the safe slamming shut). But *A Modern Instance* is very different from *Sister Carrie*, especially the ending, which is told from the point of view of the suffering Marcia. When Marcia morally triumphs and Bartley morally fails, the Christian sense of right and wrong is put in clear perspective – just as it would be if the story of Hurstwood had been told from the point of view of Mrs. Hurstwood. By telling part of the story from Hurstwood's point of view, and telling it sympathetically, Dreiser created a purely amoral world and divorced his characters from the Christian perspective around which Howells recuperated his text. Thus to read a novel like *Sister Carrie* in terms of the genteel values of Howells or the more modernistic elements of James is to read against the grain of its own working – to look for one kind of narrative ontology in a text that takes its being from a very different kind of narrative construct.

It may be that we no longer take arguments like Trilling's seriously. But we do today take comparable arguments seriously – an equally inappropriate postmodern construct is forced upon the reading of *Sister Carrie* in two recent books on literary naturalism. One of these – Walter Benn Michaels's *The Gold Standard and the Logic of Naturalism* – is basically concerned with the economic content of literary naturalism, especially as that content takes on representation within texts. Michaels considers a number of nineteenth-century novels, including *Sister Carrie*, which he reads as a novel of capitalistic desire, as opposed to an anticapitalistic novel like Howells's *The Rise of Silas Lapham*, which advocates the suppression of desire. In order to arrive at this reading, Michaels must treat a character like Robert Ames as an aberration. Michaels tells us that Ames embodied "a state of equilibrium in which one wants only what one has"[6] and equates Ames with the aesthetics of William Dean Howells.

Having negated the character of Ames, Michaels can continue with his argument, which is that men stimulate the desire for worldly goods in women like Carrie, who in turn believe that they can defy time and old age and remain eternally young by desiring the commercial goods that money represents. Michaels believes that Carrie's meaning is metaphorical or tropological: she comes to embody the spirit of capitalism, the embodiment of money and self-perpetuated desire, forms of meaning that find their physical equivalent in the corporation, which, like the futures market, is simply a fiction, a way of positioning oneself in the world. So Carrie becomes a fiction of self within the fiction of the novel – that is, she becomes a fiction of a fiction, and what she fictionalizes – the relationship between money, desire, and the fictional systems which keep them in place – explains why we so deeply identify with her as well as explaining the popularity of *Sister Carrie*.

The method of Michaels's argument, like a good deal of the new historicism, is heavily influenced by Michel Foucault. Michaels sees Dreiser's novel as a part of late nineteenth-century discourse that collapses into the discourse of capitalism and the institutions – that is, the forms of power – which hold capitalism in place. Michaels points to the fact that many critics think of Dreiser as someone outside the system he is describing. This kind of thinking, Michaels argues, turns Dreiser into a kind of God, creating a world from which he is separate. But Michaels is less clear on where we are to locate Dreiser's subjectivity within the system of capitalism. Supposedly by identifying ourselves with the objects of representation, we somehow become identical with Dreiser's own subjectivity. But the connection between and among desire, money, self, sex, writing – all supposedly related if not equivalent in the terms of the text – is really the work of the critic imposing forms of representation that embody Dreiser's mind from within capitalism, and what Michaels really gives us is his own subjectivity posing as the subjectivity of the author.

One might legitimately ask whether Michaels's readings stem from a methodology or are really part of a strategy that ends up proving what he sets out to prove. Clearly what he wants in *The Gold Standard and the Logic of Naturalism* is to come up with a series of economic readings of naturalistic texts. He has no desire to use something like the thematic approach of the New Criticism or of the old historicism. He is not interested in finding explicit references to money, gold, capitalism. His desire is to turn the idea of self into these matters, to show that the self is represented – and thus inseparable – from these terms. At this point, we no longer have need for a methodology: what we need is a strategy, and the critic negates what is contrary to his predetermined conclusion, while the text itself is turned into the tropological equivalent of capitalistic desire or whatever else the critic wants to focus on.

Thus, while Michaels spends a great deal of time talking about capitalism and desire, he spends very little time contextualizing these matters. One could argue, for example, that *Sister Carrie* is as much concerned with production as it is with consumption. When and how these matters give way to one another is something Michaels leaves untreated. Moreover, Michaels also does not make clear how he separates a kind of Foucaldian self from the consumerized self that Colin Campbell treats in his book on Romanticism and consumption.[7] Campbell argues that the kind of consumption Michaels is dealing with is a by-product of the Romantic self – the desire to turn the self into a beautiful object, the aesthetic object of its own contemplation. Carrie is far less sophisticated than Michaels suggests, however, and the connection here between self and consumption is far more tenuous than Michaels would have us believe.

An additional problem confronts us when we try to reconcile Michaels's reading of *Sister Carrie* to the way the novel narratively unfolds. *Sister Carrie*, as my own reading here has shown, is one of the most mechanistic texts that we have. Dreiser created a fictional world of almost pure causality, convinced as he was at the time by his readings of Herbert Spencer and nineteenth-century mechanistic philosophy. What Michaels fails to take into consideration is how this realm of the novel can be reconciled with his reading of free aspiration and desire. By concentrating so heavily on one trope, Michaels's reading represses as much of the narrative as it explains, and robs it of its mechanistic principles and of a causality that is built into its narrative unfolding. The strategy here thus spatializes literary form and moves narrative modes like naturalism toward the synchronic. What Michaels's reading leaves out is what is essential to literary naturalism itself: a mechanistic world view, a causal sense of sequence, a diachronic sense of time, the materialization of forms, an empirical sense of reality, and a sense of instrumentality that refuses to totalize language or to substitute aesthetics for political judgments. Here the new historicism has created a tropological, idealized, synchronic, purely formal language system to read mechanistic, causally structured, diachronic, empirically ordered texts, where language is not separated from the cultural forces and the forms of power that bring these texts into being in the first place. A new historicist reading of naturalism thus creates an incongruity between the literary text and the critical method at work, a reading that robs form of content, history of process, and language of agency – and collapses one narrative mode with great confusion into another.

Another recent reading of literary naturalism that presents similar problems is June Howard's *Form and History in American Literary Naturalism*. Howard's book is very different in attempt and scope from the Michaels book. Her concerns are with the characteristics of naturalism in relation to history. The book tends to move in three different directions – a theoretical discussion, a discussion of economic and social matters, and a series of critical readings of Dreiser, London, Norris, and Upton Sinclair.

One of the main assumptions behind Howard's book is clearly stated: "I have already rejected the notion that naturalism 'reflects' its historical period; my task is not to set literary texts against a 'history' or 'reality' whose own textuality is for that purpose repressed, but rather to trace how naturalism is shaped by and imaginatively reshapes a historical experience that, although it exists outside representation and narrative, we necessarily approach through texts."[8] The idea here is an interesting one: history does not influence the text, but rather the text influences history, becoming the prism through which we interpret our world. Central to Howard's discussion is her notion of how the text and history interpenetrate. She wants neither a formalist autotelic notion of text, nor the Aristotelian idea of the text based upon the assumption that there is some experience in reality that gets into literary texts and organizes them as genre.

Howard tells us, "Naturalism does not provide a window into reality. Rather it reveals history indirectly in revealing itself – in the significant absences silhouetted by its narratives, in the ideology invoked by the very program that proclaims a transparent access to the real, in its transmutation of content into form and form into content. The search for the real must give way to a search for the historical" (FH, 29). With this statement, Howard's argument makes a full turn, and we are back in the world of representation: she merely substitutes the idea of the historical for Walter Benn Michaels's idea of the economic. And indeed, most of her book is given over to the belief that such historical matters as immigration, poverty, and the radicalizing of America form the basis for literary naturalism, despite the fact that she also tells us that "my task is not to set literary texts against a 'history' or a 'reality'" (FH, 70). Such contradictory statements undercut Howard's arguments at the outset – contradictions she could have been spared by a theory of narrative modes. Such a theory would locate naturalism as a philosophical and literary construct, separate from physical and historical reality, but useful as a means of interpreting such reality.

4

I would like to conclude by using my reading of *Sister Carrie* to discuss another problem that has dominated recent criticism – namely, the idea of the literary text, especially the validity of the Pennsylvania Edition of *Sister Carrie*, which uses the holograph manuscript as the copy text and which deletes the coda (the ten paragraphs following Hurstwood's suicide, ending with Carrie's reflections in the rocking chair) from the novel. The basis for such a radical departure in the idea of text stems from the experience Dreiser had in getting *Sister Carrie* published. When Dreiser finished *Sister Carrie* he sent the typescript to Harper and Brothers, who rejected it on various grounds, among them that it would displease a female audience. With this in mind, the editors of the Pennsylvania Edition conjecture that Arthur Henry (Dreiser's closest friend at the time) and his wife, Jug, began to cut the novel, making changes more or less on their own.

Richard Lingeman, in his recent biography of Dreiser, agrees with the Pennsylvania editors on these points. Dreiser, according to Lingeman, "accepted all of Henry's suggestions, and they were fairly extensive – more than thirty thousand words came out." Lingeman also agrees with the Pennsylvania editors that these cuts weakened the novel by making Carrie "more of a cipher," Hurstwood a "man who remained faithful to his wife all these years, despite his coolness toward her," and Drouet less of a philanderer. Lingeman also suggests that the coda Dreiser added to the novel creates "a kind of stasis that is out of keeping with the realm of the rest of the novel."[9]

A careful look at the evidence suggests that many of these claims are mere conjecture. There is no evidence, for example, that Dreiser wanted to cut his novel based on its rejection by Harper and Brothers. There is also no evidence that Dreiser gave Henry and his wife anything like the authority claimed over the final state of his text. In fact, there is evidence to the contrary. In 1937, for exam-

81

ple, Dreiser told Louis Filler "when I finished the book, I realized that it was too long, and I went over it and marked what I thought should be cut. Then I consulted a friend, Arthur Henry, who suggested other cuts, and whenever I agreed with him I cut the book. It was thus shortened to its present length." The role of Henry and Jug in the revision of *Sister Carrie* is thus far from clear. Dreiser, we know, used Jug and Henry as amanuenses – especially Jug, who was also making a fair copy of the manuscript as the revisions went along, which shows how problematic it is to read the tracings of a foreign hand as writing independent of Dreiser. We also know that Jug's handwriting is so similar to Henry's that until recently scholars were convinced that, besides Dreiser's, there was only one hand at work. We know also that even those who see Henry as the principal agent of revisions are forced to admit, as Lingeman himself makes clear, that Henry made light pencil marks in the manuscript to suggest deletions which Dreiser had the final authority to accept or reject – an important point that often gets lost in this discussion. Added to this is the possibility that Dreiser consulted other people in the course of making revisions. Swanberg, for example, claims the influence of Mary Annabel Fanton.

I raise these questions here because I believe the whole idea of the text is a far more complex matter than the discussion of *Sister Carrie* or the discussion of textual editing in general would suggest. The main concern of textual editors has been with choosing the copy text, which then becomes the authority for the final edition. I suggest that we need to rethink the idea of the copy text as the final authority in order to supply texts of novels like *Sister Carrie* that allow readers to make judgments more consistent with the idea of narrative modes. In this context, I would like to consider at least two aspects of the novel that involve radical differences between the holograph and the first edition.

The first problem involves cuts in repetitive material. As my reading of the novel has shown, Dreiser's narrative method involved the use of repetitive sequences – as does naturalism as a narrative mode. Mechanistic philosophy depends upon the principle that all matter is in motion, subject to the physical laws of repetition. When Carrie comes to the city, she subjects herself to the laws that control the experience of the young man or woman from the country. The story of Carrie thus becomes what Kenneth Burke calls a representative anecdote, subject to a pattern of causality that leads either to success or failure. Once Dreiser decided to work within Spencer's structure of belief – that advance and decline are a part of the same mechanistic process – the story of Carrie and Hurstwood in effect became the same story. Both are influenced by the same kinds of motives – Carrie's desire for more and more becomes a corollary of Hurstwood's decline and dissolution. A textual editor thus has the problem of deciding how much repetition is justified to secure the logic of the narrative.

At some point in the history of a novel, the thinking of the author becomes at best a matter of conjecture – but such conjecture has validity if based on practical principles. One such principle involves deletions an author makes on the basis of artistic merit. A number of scenes deleted from the holograph version of *Sister Carrie* – for example, the treatment of Carrie's rise to stardom on the basis of a scowl, and a real estate agent coming to her the next day with the offer of a sumptuous Manhattan apartment practically rent-free – were excised, let us hope, because they were dramatically unconvincing. Other scenes cut from the novel – Carrie's looking for work when she becomes disillusioned with Drouet, for example – needlessly repeat her initial experience and thus impede the narrative without reinforcing it. And then there are scenes which were probably cut under the pressure of the Doubleday stipulation that Dreiser remove references to physical places – such as a very effective scene between Carrie and Drouet at Sherry's restaurant, where Ames gives a long discourse on conspicuous consumption. Only the last set of scenes should be restored because they are important to the logic of Dreiser's narrative, showing how Carrie's own ideas have been advanced through Drouet, then Hurstwood, and now through Ames, and how they anticipate the coda that Dreiser added to the final version – and which the Pennsylvania editors deleted on the flimsiest authority.

A second difference between the unrevised typescript and the first edition of the novel involves the presence of Dreiser himself in the telling of the story. In the typescript, the principal characters are very much alike – are, to put it differently, as sexually charged as Dreiser himself. In the revisions, Dreiser begins to distance himself from these characters: he makes Carrie more chaste, Drouet less repetitively the rake, and Hurstwood more reserved and mannered. Such revisions more clearly give Carrie stepping stones of desire from Drouet to Hurstwood, moving the novel more convincingly away from the middle toward the extremes embodied by Carrie's rise and Hurstwood's fall. Moreover, in diluting the narrative voice with its philosophical message, Dreiser distances himself from the story, becoming in effect more the naturalistic observer than the sentimental commentator.

All of these changes, I would argue, make *Sister Carrie* much more intelligibly consistent as literary naturalism – an object that was, I think, a kind of intuitive principle behind Dreiser's revisions. What we need, I would argue, is neither the Pennsylvania Edition nor the first edition, but a composite text in which selected cuts (perhaps in a different type) are restored to the first edition, along the lines I have just suggested. Such additions can be justified, I believe, on the grounds that they are consistent with literary naturalism as a narrative mode – that is, they bring a narrative principle to the reading, and hence the editing, of *Sister Carrie* that I believe has hitherto been lacking. As a result, we would have a *Sister Carrie* that would move much more quickly than the Pennsylvania Edition, and yet a text that would restore the revisions that Dreiser made under duress from Doubleday. Such changes would also create a much more physical sense of place and would locate the text more firmly in a historical moment. These restorations would thus be consistent with Dreiser's aim to improve his novel as a work of art and not simply to improve its chances for publication, although obviously these two desires are not mutually exclusive. Dreiser was not willing to destroy the narrative integrity of his novel – what I have been referring to as his mode of narrative discourse – to insure its publication, and this point has so far been sadly obscured, perhaps because the idea of narrative mode has played such a small part in this important discussion.

NOTES

1. Theodore Dreiser, *A Book About Myself* (New York: Boni and Liveright, 1922), p. 457.
2. Herbert Spencer, *First Principles* (New York: D. Appleton and Co., 1898), p. 199. Subsequent page references in the text (FP) are to this edition.
3. When questioned by the streetcar foreman about his credentials, Hurstwood responds, "I'm not anything" (300).
4. Walter Benjamin, *Charles Baudelaire: A Lyric Poet in the Era of High Capitalism*, trans. Harry Zohn (London: Verso, 1983).
5. Lionel Trilling, *The Liberal Imagination: Essays on Literature and Society* (Garden City, N.Y.: Doubleday, 1953).
6. Walter Benn Michaels, *The Gold Standard and the Logic of Naturalism* (Berkeley: University of California Press, 1987), p. 35.
7. Colin Campbell, *The Modern Ethic and the Spirit of Modern Consumerism* (Oxford: Blackwell, 1987).
8. June Howard, *Form and History in American Literary Naturalism* (Chapel Hill: University of North Carolina, 1985), p. 70. Subsequent page references in the text (FH) are to this volume.
9. Richard Lingeman, *Theodore Dreiser: At the Gates of the City, 1871–1907* (New York: G. P. Putnam's Sons, 1986), pp. 280, 278.

Who Narrates? Dreiser's Presence in *Sister Carrie*

ALAN TRACHTENBERG

> He is no philosopher.
> His only gift is to enact
> All that his deepest self abhors,
> And learn, in his self-contempting distress,
> The secret worth
> Of all our human worthlessness.
> —Robert Penn Warren

1

WHY has *Sister Carrie* so resolutely defied interpretation? Born into controversy when its original publisher tried to cancel its contract in 1900 – the whole episode exaggerated by Dreiser into a notorious scandal of suppression – the novel has yet to free itself altogether from the fate of exemplifying a life or a cultural moment.[1] Few scholars dispute its importance – but as an event in the history of American mores and morals more than as a novel interesting for being just that: a work of fiction. Signs of change have appeared recently, including disagreements over what the novel may mean. Is the book for or against capitalism? Is it as sentimental as it often sounds? And the "bad" writing every critic, even the friendliest, has deplored – is it perhaps intentionally bad, Dreiser's effort at parody of the language of "false consciousness" to highlight a style of "realism" as antidote to the romantic pap, the "linguistic junk of commodified language" bred by consumer capitalism? What are the generic relations between "romance" and "realism" in the book? Recent readers have been prone to see the book as a battleground of styles, of genres, of ideologies, and to ask what *Sister Carrie* might mean for us today as a text of its own times.[2]

The issue high on many scholarly agendas today is "representation." How does *Sister Carrie* portray its world, its characters, the springs of action within that world, itself as an action within the setting it projects in such extensive detail – what F. O. Matthiessen called "solid slabs of continuous experience?"[3] Critics of representation typically seek the revealing detail, the suspiciously self-contradictory passage; in a novel like Dreiser's they naturally focus on description – all those details about railroad journeys, city streets, department stores, Shore Drive mansions, the Broadway promenade, Bowery flophouses, elegant New York theatres and hotels. They seek patterns – of motion, performance, speech, characterization, and have opened the texture of the text to new meticulous investigation.[4]

Representation conceived as description leaves unresolved the more difficult and opaque question of the novel as *narrative,* a *form* of action, the construction of point of view, a built arrangement of "scenes" and "pictures," to employ the Jamesian terms systematized by Percy Lubbock as aspects of the "craft of fiction."[5] Narrative also "represents," and *Sister Carrie* is before anything else a *story* told in a certain way – a way of story telling which shapes how we know what is being represented and how.

Is the form of *Sister Carrie* interesting enough to challenge analysis and interpretation? I think so; for nothing about the novel is more important, even culturally and historically, than its invention of a new way of telling a new American story – a new form for a new content. Of course a wall of prejudice stands in the way of a formalist (even a historically formalist) reading of this inaugural novel by a former newspaperman. Between Dreiser and the "craft of fiction" there has seemed to be little commerce. "Dreiser had no intention of creating anything like a Jamesian 'house of fiction,' " wrote Richard Poirier some twenty five years ago. "The shape of the material was the shape for the most part merely of his recollections. Writing for him obviously did not involve the 'building' of a world so much as reporting on one already existent."[6] More recent studies show that recurring patterns of images and actions – imagery of water, weather, doors, windows, rocking chairs, and acts of drifting, glimpsing, rocking – cannot be ignored as at least rudimentary signs of a motive to build rather than merely to recollect, as do more subtle foreshadowings, anticipations, and fragmentary but distinct elements of plot (coincidences, withheld information, deceptions, snatches of memory, even elements of crisis and *peripeteia*).[7]

Discussions of form in *Sister Carrie* have rarely ventured beyond the rise-and-fall pattern which dominates the New York half of the narrative (although Carrie's ascent and Hurstwood's decline begin their respective accumulations of momentum in Chicago), or the "plotting of inarticulate experience," by which Julian Markels meant, in an important essay in 1961, Dreiser's skillful method of arranging episodes "in order to dramatize with perfect coherence that absence of foreordained purpose in the universe, and its corollary, the hegemony of chance, of which he speaks so awkwardly in his 'philosophical' writings."[8] Markels concedes that Dreiser's "bad" writing (his "thick prose") coexists with his "good," and concludes that the author's "method of construction, which is his true source of strength," is "also his source of weakness," for it "disables Dreiser from portraying the emergence in human experience of moral consciousness and its corollary, literary style."[9]

Style has been the sticking point in efforts to pinpoint the narrative form of *Sister Carrie*. "Granted that he often writes as if language itself were a bore," Richard Poirier remarks, echoing F. R. Leavis, "there remains the mystery of Dreiser's undeniable power over the imagination of even his severest critics" (WE 240). Talk of power and mystery, somehow connected with boring, slovenly writing, can still be heard in Dreiser criticism – a continuing sign, surely, of a still unresolved ambivalence toward this author and this novel, both from the other side of the tracks, so to speak, of the Jamesian house in which well-crafted fiction thrives among its other Anglo-Saxon and well-off inhabitants. Poirier himself provides a superb example, for as damning as are his remarks about Dreiser's disregard for writing good English and crafting fine fiction, the critic makes a dazzling about-face and finds virtue in all the alleged defects.

The view of Poirier's which I find at once most compelling and most mistaken concerns the role of Dreiser himself, or of his narrator-surrogate, within the novel. Dreiser refuses to give a clear characterization of *himself* in the book, Poirier observes – refuses to say where he stands in relation to his characters and his readers.

The "fluctuations of voice" page after page represent a perverse self-fragmentation. Dreiser provides "no plastic coherence among the lurid varieties of self-characterization that emerge from his language." And all this is to the good, for "the fractured characterization Dreiser gives of himself as narrator of *Sister Carrie* is evidence of the integrity of his vision" (WE 240).

Poirier's views of the fractured narrator and of the integrity of vision are both, I believe, contestable despite their elegance. Contesting the first issue by showing a "plastic coherence" among the narrator's several voices will not be easy in a brief essay – indeed, to make the argument hold, nothing less than a page-by-page exegesis would do. My aim here can be only a suggestive argument, not a final one. The second issue inspires more confidence. Dreiser's is a vision, Poirier argues, "in which character – as a derivative of language and the power of language – is regarded as negligible" (WE 240). For Poirier the incoherence of narrative voice is the very sign of the coherence of the novel's asocial vision, its negation of the bourgeois ideology of the English novel, the vision whereby selves and societies are made by "characters" engaged in purposeful and self-reflective acts of language – in short, in conversation. Determined not to write a traditional novel, Dreiser "seems not even to care about achieving through language any shaped social identity." He simply rejects "those conversational involvements that imply that the self or society is formed by intensities of personal effort" (WE 240). More interested in "environmental force" than in "character," as the realists understood that fictive concept,[10] Dreiser is best – and very good indeed – when he deals with "things," "the objects that fill what were the free spaces of America" (WE 249).

The challenge, then, is to see if the narrative voice of *Sister Carrie* does in fact make itself discontinuous and incoherent, and if it indeed treats character – in the sense of intersubjective relations mediated by language – as, in Poirier's word, "negligible."

Writing several years before Poirier, William J. Handy also argued that "the most immediate impression" of *Sister Carrie* "is that of the looming presence of Dreiser throughout the work."[11] But rather than fractured or incoherent, Handy sees Dreiser as an "unseen presence" who "integrates his own point of view with that of

90

his characters" (H 523). How he achieves this – how, line by line, he insinuates his own point of view upon that of Carrie, complementing her limited self-awareness with his own more worldly knowledge, holds "the key to the effective artistic meaning of the novel" (H 525). "The ultimate effect becomes in *Sister Carrie* the expression of the powerful, omniscient presence of Dreiser, an integral part of every action, every attitude, every implicit and expressed value" (H 524).

Few critics have heeded Handy's extravagant but provocative point. Handy's most radical suggestion is that Dreiser installs himself as something more than or different from a technically omniscient narrator; he puts himself in the narrative as a subjective presence. The formal effect is to create for the reader a standpoint at once within and without Carrie's self-awareness – to hear and even speak her words in our silent mouthings of the text, while at once hearing and speaking another voice which comprehends what Carrie does not know of herself and cannot utter. And the final or totalizing effect for Handy is that the Dreiserian voice represents an "integration of self and art" (H 525) – what Ames helps Carrie realize, and which at the end Carrie moves tentatively toward.

Handy's argument that Dreiser's narrative voice represents "authenticity as an expressive symbol" deserves to be cited directly:

> . . . the literary power lies in the singular way Dreiser's sensibility, as that sensibility inheres in every scene, acts to become an expressive symbol for artistic meaning. What is meant by Dreiser's sensibility is his felt, rather than formulated, values – those values which produce his own special responsiveness to the pathetic in life, his special kind of caring for mankind, his honest, his acute awareness of social cruelty, his sometimes reverential, sometimes bewildered, reaction to the way of life in America. It is this integration of self and art which produces the voice of Dreiser. (H 525)

The narrative voice presents itself, according to this eloquent view of Dreiserian pity and insight, as the needed alternative to the language of his "inarticulate" characters – to Carrie's especially, for she is Dreiser's own double, his shadow or surrogate.[12]

Handy and Poirier together help pose the problem I want to explore here: how the narrative voice functions in specific passages; whether fluctuations or discontinuities may be taken as facets of one voice, a controlling narrative agency which may be the main thing, the real point of interest in the novel. What *Sister Carrie* means, what it means in its own history and in ours, even what the novel is really *about*: these unsettled questions have quickened the contemporary life of this novel, especially in the present climate of historicist criticism. Character and society (or what constitutes "the social") are cognate issues, and throw open the door to historical interpretation of the novel, how it depicts its social world, how it understands the construction of character and of the social dimension of experience under the conditions of life it sets in motion. Analysis of the narrative voice, its distinctive role as a presence – its role in *socializing* the narrative – is what I explore here, with the prospect that reading the narrator back into the novel may help us read the novel itself back into its history, and make it more meaningfully available to our own.

2

Toward the close of Chapter 1, as the train nears Chicago and Carrie tentatively responds to Drouet's gambit, "You'll be at home if I come around Monday night?" with "I think so" – they had just exchanged names and addresses and certain unspoken intimations – another voice, neither Carrie's nor Drouet's, enters the scene:

> How true it is that words are but vague shadows of the volumes we mean. Little audible links, they are, chaining together great inaudible feelings and purposes. (6)

This is not the first authorial intervention in the opening chapter; recall the Balzacian observations as early as the third paragraph. There the author's narrative voice ironizes the familiar sentimental/evangelical text, "the city has its cunning wiles" (1), and sets up polarities ("better," "worse") which melodramatically predefine the possible fate of "a girl [who] leaves home at eighteen." These polarities present in the simplest, boldest, and apparently most sincere form the very terms the subsequent narrative will transvalue. Of course we cannot yet anticipate the narrative role of the better/worse syndrome, but it is not long (in the following Chicago chapters) before we realize that Carrie may well turn out "better" at the end for having been "worse" at the beginning – better, that is, in the transvalued perspective the narrative will meticulously, often laboriously, construct in the course of the novel. The method of constructing a new perspective upon these old terms of popular/sentimental/evangelical judgment on country girls leaving home for the big city includes interventions such as this passage about words as vague shadows of meanings, to which we shall shortly return.

Early in Chapter 1 we cannot yet foretell the terms of a transvalued "bettering" process – though the direction is anticipated by the remark in the fourth paragraph, that "Books were beyond her interest – knowledge a sealed book" (2), which we may recall at the end of the novel when we see Carrie, discontented in her success, reading *Père Goriot* (363). Balzac had been recommended to her by Ames, whose "ideals burned in her heart" (293), and the effect of the story of Rastignac's pursuit of love and success in Paris was "That for the first time, it was being borne in upon her how silly and worthless had been her earlier reading, as a whole" (363). In the original manuscript Dreiser had made explicit the significance of Balzac to Carrie's own desires for an elusive happiness. The original passage has Carrie speak of the sadness of Lucien de Rubempré in *The Great Man from the Provinces:*

> "Yes," he [Ames] answered, "if a man doesn't make knowledge his object, he's very likely to fail. He didn't fail in anything but love and fortune, and that isn't everything. Balzac makes too much of those things. He wasn't any poorer in mind when he left Paris than when he came to it. In fact he was richer, if he had only thought so. Failure in love isn't so much."
>
> "Oh, don't you think so?" asked Carrie, wistfully.
>
> "No. It is the man who fails in his mind who fails completely. Some people get the idea that their happiness lies in wealth and position. Balzac thought so, I believe. Many people do . . ." (482 Penn)

These deleted lines clarify (perhaps too obviously) the significance of the Balzac text Carrie reads at the end – a sign not just of superior reading habits, but the beginnings of the habit of *critical* reading by which she reflects upon her own experience by means of "serious" reading. Her response to *Père Goriot* suggests that at the end she had begun to unseal the book of knowledge.

In Chapter 1, however, Carrie's train ride to Chicago falls squarely within the pattern of the melodrama of moralistic worsening. Like the master of disguise in the evangelical ur-melodrama of "better" and "worse," the cunning city "appeal[s] to the astonished senses in equivocal terms. . . . what falsehoods may not these *things* breath into the unguarded ear!" (2; emphasis supplied) The appeal of the city *speaks* through *things*, and we are prepared at once for the proliferation of "voices" in this text. "'That,' said a voice in her ear, 'is one of the prettiest little resorts in Wisconsin'" (2) is unmistakably a voice performing the role of tempter, the city's wiles in the guise of a sweet-talking tongue. As soon as she replies "Is it?" Carrie's career of conventional worsening has begun, and the narrator's self-assumed task, implied by his ironic tone in the third paragraph, is to subvert that judgment, to convert it slowly, painstakingly, cumulatively into another perspective, the complex point of view of the full narrative as it unfolds.

The city has many wiles, and Drouet represents only the initial voice that Carrie will encounter. His whisper in her ear suggests an allegorical role; but Drouet is of course a fully actual person, a historical being whose role in the melodrama of the opening paragraphs derives from an image of himself internalized from such images as are available in his culture, an image of such a man as he imagines himself to be. His voice in Carrie's ear bespeaks a historical character expressed and particularized by those unconscious allegorical shadings in his whispering voice. And her "unguarded" ear itself implies a history, for it is only a partially innocent ear; we have already learned in the fourth paragraph of Carrie's readiness to assume the role of "half-equipped little knight," a role scripted by the popular melodrama infiltrating an emerging urban commercial culture in just the years covered by the novel, the late 1880s and 1890s – a culture produced for mass consumption, of sentimental magazine fiction, costume historical romances, staged melodramas and musical reviews, popular ballads on sentimental themes (of which Dreiser's brother, Paul Dresser, was one of the most celebrated authors).[13]

The flirtation-seduction scene on the train replicates the conventionality of the sermon parodied in the third paragraph (we will soon learn how continuously present in the narrative will be allusions to the moral polarities, the "better" and "worse" of the evangelical-sentimental melodrama by which life imitated art in the middle regions of turn-of-the-century culture in America). After a few paragraphs of idle talk about resorts and hotels (Carrie's initiation into the *spoken* acknowledgment of such sites of pleasure), the narrative voice once more intervenes, this time in the guise of the social historian who will be available throughout the ensuing narrative not just to assure the reader that the story plays itself out on a ground of reliable fact, but more important, to sharpen the reader's attention to a dialectical tension between historical fact and theatricalized and sentimental illusion. The omniscient narrator provides social information – Carrie's mind and her social class, for instance, as "a fair example of the middle American class" (2), or Drouet as "a type of the travelling canvasser for a manufacturing house" (3). These details help us see the flirtation in progress in historical-social as well as personal terms: a male salesman who is also a "masher" (another historical "type") playing up to a naive but self-interested country girl "quick to understand the keener pleasures of life, ambitious to gain in material things" (2) – in short, prepared by an implied socialization already in process to enter the city as an eager consumer of the personal goods Drouet's vocation signifies: the flood of personal goods into the urban market which was one of the distinctive characteristics of the 1890s.[14]

"Lest this order of individual should permanently pass," the narrator adds to his account of the "drummer" and the "masher" – terms which had appeared "at that time" (we have already learned in the opening paragraph that the time is "August, 1889") – "let me put down some of the most striking characteristics of his most successful manner and method" (3). By the conventional literary politeness of "let me" the Dreiserian narrator plants himself within the text, becomes the implied "I" of the narrative ("I" will appear literally in Chapter 33 where the narrator distinguishes between "the higher mental development" and "the common type of mind" [241]), thus qualifying, though inconspicuously, his claim to omniscience, to a privileged place in the narrative from which he might speak (as historian, for example) with unchallengeable objectivity. At this early stage of the narrative whatever ambiguity attaches to "let me" and the implied presence of a narrating *character* barely causes a ripple. The third person referent, "his," introduces a more immediately functional ambiguity. The pronoun clearly designates Drouet, but Drouet as a *type* and thus also not-Drouet. The voice in Carrie's ear now appears as both himself and not-himself, a person and a social type. His representivity as "drummer" and "masher" grounds his *personal* identity, places him in the reader's *social* cognition, recognizes him as a creature of a collective history (the word "type" implies that there are countless more like him). Throughout Drouet remains "the drummer," Carrie the "little toiler" and "the shop girl" or "that little soldier of fortune," and Hurstwood "the manager" and "the ex-manager." Introduced by the voice of omniscience – what the unobtrusive narrator can be assumed properly to know about his characters and their situations – social representivity and its historical origins becomes contrapuntal to the popular moral allegory in the narrative perspective, whose complication begins at once in Chapter 1.

In these early passages of intervention the narrator's point of view poses no problem. The narrator as historian fills in or documents social facts to be absorbed by the reader as signs not only of the specific social character of the individual named Drouet (his ontological dependency on the larger categorical name "drummer"), but as signs too of the social constitution of the entire fictive world in which the story unfolds: the fact that the immediate sensory world is a *society* in which individuals, at least from a perspective above and beyond their own self-realization (their roles within the internalized melodrama they imagine as their "real" and "free" beings), represent types or classes, countless absent others. As the narrative progresses, more inward meanings of "social" will appear, but here, in this early intervention, the chosen method, drawn from the repertoire of the nineteenth-century realistic novel, takes the form of an omniscient narrative voice exercising itself from beyond and behind the subjectivities of the introduced characters.

Not until the two sentences about words as shadows of meanings which appear as the train nears Chicago do we catch something significantly different in Dreiser's narrative voice – a commentary which establishes a new relation between narrative voice and narrative event. The opening sentences of a paragraph of reflection on the exchange of names and addresses and the tentative date for Monday night, the lines momentarily draw the reader's attention away, for the first time in the chapter, from the immediate scene toward an idea in the form of a general proposition, in this case an idea embodied in figurative images of shadows, links, chains. The rough meaning seems obvious enough: spoken words reveal only partially what people really feel and mean. That idea had been planted two pages earlier:

> There was much more passing now than the mere words indicated. He recognized the indescribable thing that made up for fascination and beauty in her. She realized that she was of interest to him from the one standpoint which a woman both delights in and fears. (5)

In this case the narrator supplements the "mere words" of Drouet and Carrie by claiming his privilege of omniscience to tell us directly and authoritatively what, from the narrative point of view, *he* knows: what Drouet "recognized" (something "indescribable") and what Carrie "realized" (her ambivalent response to her perception of his "interest").

Now, as the train nears Chicago, Dreiser expostulates in a different voice coming from a different location upon the implication of "mere words," a two-sentence metaphoric discourse on language and meaning. Here he exceeds the normal privilege of omniscience. He introduces a voice as if from *inside* the narration (recalling the now silently implied "let me"), yet registered in a tone and diction quite different from that of the narrative proper.

It will be useful to pause here to clarify the technical features of Dreiser's rather sudden appearance in a different voice at just this juncture. We can call upon the distinctions between "narrative" and "discourse" Gerard Genette draws from the linguistic theorist Emile Benveniste, the "opposition between the objectivity of narrative and the subjectivity of discourse. Narrative objectivity means "the absence of any reference to the narrator," or as Benveniste puts it: "As a matter of fact, there is then no longer even a narrator. The events are set forth chronologically, as they occur. No one speaks here; the events seem to narrate themselves." If narrative is apparently autonomous, discourse is dependent upon a distinct speaker.

> In discourse, someone speaks, and his situation in the very act of speaking is the focus of the most important significations; in narrative, as Benveniste forcefully puts it, *no one speaks*, in the sense that at no moment do we ask ourselves *who is speaking, where, when,* and so forth, in order to receive the full signification of the text.

The relations between narrative and discourse, Genette observes, remain in balance in "the classical age of objective narration, from Balzac to Tolstoy," but change radically in the modern period.[15]

To ask "who is speaking" in the Dreiserian discursive passages is to find oneself wrestling precisely with the problem Poirier and Handy raise: the actual presence of a figure called "Dreiser" within the narrative. If he is there, then discourse has its clear, unequivocal source, its *someone.* If he is not there as such, then the voice of discourse is equivocal, a problematic posed by the "fluctuating voices" of the narrative. Although he seems to want to employ a signified authorial discourse – direct intervention in his own person – in a manner closer to that of Fielding than to that of, say, Howells, Dreiser remains essentially within the classical mode of "objective narration." He attempts to keep narrative and discourse separate, though his discursive appearances often also narrate or "recount," as Genette argues that discourse by its nature can do – that is, they can narrate from within the mode of discourse, in *someone's* voice (this identity of a speaker distinguishing discursive narration from objective narration proper). Dreiser's exploitation of the inherent impurity of discourse, as Genette describes it, indicates the hybrid nature of his narrative voice – which in turn suggests his attempt to accommodate his narrative to a new novelistic subject matter, a new point of view toward his material and his reader, and a new historical situation for American fiction. The unusual character of Dreiser's narrative in *Sister Carrie,* as both Poirier and Handy in their different ways apprehend it, derives from an innovative fusion of narrative and discourse, an equivocal and premodernist reordering of the priorities of the two modes – for the sake, it seems likely, of allowing the novice author greater freedom to make the story he recounts both its own and *his* own story: the story of his subjective experience of it mediating the story proper.

The discursive paragraph in question opens with two separate tropes which together comprise a strangely but not incoherently mixed metaphor. Then the passage returns to the interrupted scene which is presumed to have remained in progress during the narrator's subjective commentary – that is to say, not so much interrupted but momentarily turned away from, as in a dramatic aside by a choric speaker:

> How true it is that words are but vague shadows of the volumes we mean. Little audible links, they are, chaining together great inaudible feelings and purposes. Here were these two, bantering little phrases, drawing purses, looking at cards, and both unconscious of how inarticulate all their real feelings were. Neither was wise enough to be sure of the working of the mind of the other. He could not tell how his luring succeeded. She could not realize that she was drifting, until he secured her address. Now she felt that she had yielded something – he, that he had gained a victory. Already they felt that they were somehow associated. Already he took control in directing the conversation. His words were easy. Her manner was relaxed. (6)

The opening figures – words, shadows, volumes, links, chains – give the reader pause, require more than a quick reading to parse. As an ensemble of tropes they elicit from the reader an act of semantic analysis drawing attention away from the ongoing narrative they pedantically comment upon. Moreover, instead of clearly signified meanings we find ourselves amid ambiguous alternative meanings. What do volumes (material books? an immaterial quantity of space?) have in common with chains, which might imprison and isolate as much as join together? If volumes refer to books, do chains made up of word-links (whose relation to meaning is both shadowy and inaudible) imply sentences, lexical chains, of which books – this book we hold in hand, for instance – consist? Do the metaphors, then, warn us not to take the meanings of this very novel as exactly cognate with the actual words on the page, but urge us instead to attend to "great inaudible feelings and purposes" which lie somewhere beyond the written words yet "linked" to them, as shadows are metonymically linked or joined as traces (what Charles Sanders Peirce calls "indices") of their material source? The vague shadow of a meaning reveals at least that meaning is somewhere in the vicinity, if not exactly *in* or identical to the lexical signification of the exact word casting the shadow. Why does Dreiser introduce such apparent skepticism, which might well be taken as a reflection upon his own novelistic purposes, at just the point when Carrie's "I think so" expresses such an ambiguously indecisive response to the masher's advances – unless he wished readers to draw an analogy between the small but portentous talk passing between Carrie and Drouet and his own conversation, as narrator, with the reader?

One implication of the metaphoric figure is that words resemble or behave like *things;* they share density and mass, cast shadows, and possess autonomous force enough to combine themselves into chains. The metaphor thus plants an unconscious association we have already encountered in the fourth paragraph, where things breathe falsehoods into unguarded ears, and which we will encounter explicitly, in another passage of discourse, in a later chapter. True, the metaphors explain little about the logical or semiotic relation between words and meanings, except to imply that the relation is ambiguous. Words are only partial signs; their thing-like power lies precisely in this, in their imprecision – in what their ambiguity brings forth as absences, palpable half-disclosures like shadows, like those "little phrases" bandied back and forth between Carrie and Drouet the "real feelings" of which they are "unconscious." The discursive voice intervenes in order to translate that felt absence, not into precise lexical meaning, but into precisely rendered imprecision – what "he could not tell," what "she could not realize." (We will see later how the narrator makes his motive and function of "translation" explicit.)

The metaphoric discourse on novelistic language, on spoken words and inchoate meanings, coheres, then, into an observation absorbed back into the narrative proper as a discourse on conscious and unconscious meanings, chiefly on the failure of intention to achieve either silent or spoken articulation. It is striking, especially to readers accustomed to thinking of *Sister Carrie* as a "naturalist" narrative concerned almost entirely with "externalities," to discover how much attention in the opening chapter (and throughout the novel) the narrator devotes to what each character is "conscious" of, what each "knew" of the other's mind. The second paragraph in the original manuscript begins, "To be sure she was not conscious of any of this" (that the threads binding her to girlhood and home "were irretrievably broken" by the departure described in the first paragraph) (3 Penn). Just after Drouet appears as a "voice in her ear" we learn that "for some time she had been conscious of a man behind" (2), and after their opening chit-chat we read: "All the time she was conscious of certain features out of the side of her eye" (3). We learn very early Carrie's capacity to dissemble, to pretend *not to be* conscious, to seem unconcerned and unaware – as she does again in the chapter's final paragraph when, in company with her sister, she exchanges a covert look with Drouet (8).

The local relevance of the commentary is clear enough:[16] neither of the characters possesses sufficient self-consciousness, powers of articulation, or wisdom to understand just what is happening in the little drama they are enacting. Both are engaged in the playing of roles, in small dissemblings, rehearsed performances; they are actors uncertain of their scripts (Drouet less so), though we as readers can plainly enough see a conventionally melodramatic flirtation-seduction in progress.[17] Both are "unconscious of how inarticulate all their real feelings were," yet they play at expressing or withholding feelings. "Neither was wise enough to be sure of the working of the mind of the other."

Unconscious, inarticulate, real feelings, the working of the mind of the other: they are key terms in the novel as a whole, terms Dreiser returns to again and again to confirm the narrative strategy initiated in the opening chapter, and to suggest, again surprisingly, that *consciousness* is precisely what this novel is largely about – a notion of consciousness which remarkably resembles that which William James developed in the same years. According to James, consciousness is (1) the *experience* of thought, rather than an abstract capacity as such, and (2) inseparable from the world of things which we speak of being conscious *of*. Dreiser's thingness of words and the wordness (or articulateness) of things, rendered by the narrator as voices, corresponds closely to James's argument that thoughts and things, rather than different substances, represent different functions, different experiences of the same nameless thing.[18] Thus Dreiser's typical discursive practice of departing from narrative proper at certain key points reveals a consistent motive: to provide in direct address to the reader (as discourse) an account (often figurative, in tropes of water, tides, weather, and so on) of inner experience, of intersubjective awareness of the other, which neither Carrie nor Drouet nor Hurstwood is capable of supplying in a conversational or meditational voice – yet which constitutes the form and content of each character's self-awareness. They cannot say so for themselves; it takes the narrator to say it to us for them.

3

Dreiser adapts his narrative voice in *Sister Carrie* to structural and formal needs he created for himself by introducing into American fiction a certain kind of character of limited self-reflection and self-knowledge. His characters are not devoid of thought altogether, and as I have suggested, the novel devotes a surprising amount of attention to mind and consciousness, to "mental process," to what people do and do not *know*.[19] Certainly no one can deny that Dreiser departed, as Poirier argued, from the conception of character which shaped the nineteenth-century realistic novel – as much in Howells and James, we should add, as in the English novelists. James provides one *locus classicus* of the ideal self of realistic fiction: "Experience, as I see it, is our apprehension and our measure of what happens to us as social creatures – any intelligent report of which has to be based on that apprehension."[20] Characters unable to provide intelligent reports are by that measure ruled out as viable characters: "We care, our curiosity and our sympathy care comparatively little for what happens to the stupid, the coarse and the blind." It is the "really sentient" who matter for novelists: "the figures in any picture, the agents in any drama, are interesting only in proportion as they feel their respective situations; since the consciousness, on their part, of the complication exhibited forms for us their link or connection with it."[21]

It takes little more than a paragraph or two in *Sister Carrie* for the reader to learn that Dreiser's characters are not of this sort, not "really sentient," and if interesting at all, can not be so "only in proportion as they feel their respective situations" and are able to articulate their feelings in conversation, or as in Isabel Archer's great "vigil" in chapter 42 of *Portrait of a Lady*, in which sheer analysis and self-reflection in silent meditation lead Isabel to at once intellectual and emotional realizations about her complex entrapment. Compare Carrie's "doubts and misgivings" (160) after returning from the walk in the park with Hurstwood during which she accepted his pledge of marriage in exchange for her abandoning the drummer for the manager. Carrie too faces a dilemma based on a deception she has not yet figured out – Hurstwood's being already married – and the narrator represents her inner reflections as a wavering between two conflicting interests in her feelings: the anticipated pleasure of Hurstwood's passion (the discursive narrative voice reveals that the passion lacks "majesty" but is strong enough to bend Carrie in Hurstwood's direction) against the anticipated loss of the comfort she already enjoys with Drouet, should the Hurstwood affair not work out. "She might have been said," the narrator discloses, "to be imagining herself in love, when she was not" (161). Capable only of experiencing herself in a state of indecision, Carrie cannot take the next step toward the awesome realization the narrator has just shared with the reader. The interest one takes in Carrie arises largely from recognitions shared by the narrator of her *inadequacy* to her situation – how even in success she remains lost to her own motives, unable to think through the consequences of her actions and arrive at self-knowledge, a sensible experience of her own being. It is this inadequacy which, by means of his hybrid narrative-discursive method, Dreiser translates into the reader's experience, which gives Carrie life as a character, encourages us to participate as empathetic witnesses in the transvaluation of the terms "better" and "worse" working themselves out in the process of her slowly awakening self-presence.

The radical break *Sister Carrie* represented in American realism lay at least superficially in its aggressively offensive content – the absence, as Randolph Bourne put it perfectly, of any hint of moral "redemption" (or punishment) in a story about a "fallen" woman who trades her virginity to a shallow but good-natured "drummer" for a roof over her head, good food and fancy clothes, then runs off with a saloon manager (a few steps up the social ladder) who turns out to be married (nevertheless she willingly marries him in an invalid ceremony), deserts him as his luck runs out in New York, makes her success as a show girl, and still holds our sympathy at the end as, comfortable in her flat at the Waldorf, she reads *Père Goriot* and dreams of an ever-elusive happiness.[22] The absence of redemption implies too the absence of *plot* (as distinct from the topographical "plotting of inarticulate experience"). The relative weakness of plot in *Sister Carrie,* of extended complications through which sentient characters work through their relations to each other and to themselves by means of memory and intelligence, follows as much from the kind of characters Dreiser chose to depict as from his distrust of the neatly rounded-off endings of popular romances.

But the external facts alone of the story fail to capture the more troubling features of this novel, which provoked reviews such as this: "The book is a dangerous one, the story of lives steeped in sin and degradation. There is not one sentence to redeem the sordid tale of the sickening life of men and women who pass before the public as honored members of society."[23] The story's cast of characters offended as much as its amorality – characters drawn neither from the top (as in Henry James) nor the bottom (as in Stephen Crane) nor the respectable upper middle (as in William Dean Howells), but from a new middle range which had emerged in the last decades of the nineteenth century within new social institutions transforming popular life in the larger American cities.[24] It was his choice, more Balzacian than Howellsian, to tell a story of *popular* life from a new, untried perspective – unless we take as precedents the mid-century writings of Poe, Lippard, Whitman, and Melville in his city writings[25] – that sharpened Dreiser's break with the realism of Howells. For the perspective he chose was essentially from *within* the popular, the demotic, the vulgar – not the life of the "working masses" (they are only glimpsed) but of successful representatives of new social types appearing in a new phase of urban industrial capitalism, the first generation in the first era of mass consumerism who took the pursuit of material happiness as their everyday goal and dream.[26] Consider the social origins, the social typicality, of the leading players: Carrie, a country girl who seeks escape in the city from the proletarian fate of her family; Drouet, a "travelling canvasser for a manufacturing house" just at the time when American industrial capitalism was turning to aggressive marketing techniques and advertising to create mass appetites for goods, for consumable commodities; Hurstwood, manager of "a truly swell saloon" in Chicago, whose skills of "creating a good impression" (33) or what we would call image-management, are keyed to those finely graded social distinctions on display in the new urban sites of male entertainment and recreation. "Altogether a very acceptable individual of our great American upper class – the first grade below the luxuriously rich" (34), Hurstwood stands for the inherent instability of individual stations within a new social order based on visible tokens of prestige and celebrity.

Sister Carrie depicts, moreover, a world not of work but of play: the city at night, with its own system of time measurable in digits of pleasure (equivalent to the expenditure of cash) – the city of electric lights diurnally countermanding the strictly measured temporal system of daylight hours, of piecework or wage labor in factory or retail shop. As the train enters Chicago at the close of Chapter 1 the narrator portrays, in images that provide an analogue to just the feelings coursing wordlessly through Carrie's senses, the sphere in which his story will take place – which indeed it has already entered, through the aura Drouet has cast upon Carrie's imagination:

> . . . that mystic period between the glare and gloom of the world when life is changing from one sphere or condition to the next. Ah, the promise of the night. What does it not hold for the weary! What old illusion of hope is not here forever repeated! Says the soul of the toiler to itself, "I shall soon be free. I shall be in the ways and the hosts of the merry. The streets, the lamps, the lighted chamber set for dining, are for me. The theatre, the halls, the parties, the ways of rest and the paths of song – these are mine in the night." Though all humanity be still enclosed in the shops, the thrill runs abroad. It is in the air. The dullest feel something which they may not always express or describe. It is the lifting of the burden of toil. (7)

The diction of this crucial paragraph seems lifted straight from popular magazine fiction – an example of the sentimentality and melodrama for which Dreiser is regularly faulted. "What old illusion of hope is not here forever repeated!" seems so much at odds with the actual facts of Chicago nightlife related in a more straight-forward narrative style later on – the petty games of conspicuous display and womanizing, the sordidness behind Hurstwood's fastidiously polished facade, the crude sexual advances Carrie encounters as she seeks a footing in the theatre business, the dark underside of the city at night through which Hurstwood prowls in search of food and shelter – that the language seems at least retrospectively ironic.

But the popular melody Dreiser sings in this passage conveys by tone and lilt precisely what the "wholly untravelled" Carrie would feel on the train as she "gazed out of the window" (one of her characteristic gestures throughout the novel, looking out or looking in toward something which arouses desire) as evening turns to night in the city. The triteness itself provides an Eliot-like correlative to Carrie's inarticulate point of view. Dreiser's gift is to make the trite seem credible, stirring in its own right even as we recognize its tinsel quality. The device of ascribing a voice to desire – what the "soul of the toiler" says "to itself" – gives the "old illusion of hope" a concrete social meaning: what those "still enclosed in shops" anticipate as release and relief when the clock which measures units of labor ceases, when night seems to cancel all clocks and makes play and pleasure seem timeless. Moreover, the narrator-ventriloquist's rendering of the toiler's soul's speech deepens the social meaning by allowing us to recognize the core illusion of the city's promise of pleasure-for-cash: the illusion that "the streets, the lamps, the lighted chamber set for dining, are *for me*" [emphasis supplied], that the city's promise of freedom and enjoyment is "mine in the night," that "I" exist at night as a "free" being, an inverted mirror image of my daytime unfreedom "enclosed in the shops" (7). Reversing the values of night and day, darkness and light, the city with its artificial illumination inverts darkness into ironic freedom, freedom to claim the world of goods as "*mine* in the night" [emphasis supplied]. Yet the electric lights of the city night hide the truth which appears with each break of dawn: the shops, the toil, the clocks, the mechanical labor Carrie will experience in the shoe factory, as the price of her nighttime illusions of freedom.

106

4

Dreiser's choice to depict a new American milieu at the moment of its emergence, a milieu he understood from within (because he was also able to see it from without: the double act of novelistic imagination his hybrid narrative intends to perform) as a compendium of historical process and psycho-cultural consciousness – a history consisting of both material facts and immaterial fancies, dreams, and desires – obliged him to devise a new narrative form, to revise the form of Howellsian realism, to abandon the narrative of moral dilemma along with the moral universe and what Wai Chee Dimock has recently defined brilliantly as the "economy of pain" by which realism proffered its middle-class reassurances.[27] Dreiser needed to accommodate his form to a content which lay beyond the boundaries of acceptable representation – the content of his own milieu, his inside vision of it: nightclubs, saloons, gambling, fast women, guiltless illicit sexuality, vulgar obsession with fashionable clothes, expensive eating places, and popular musical shows; an uncultivated, comfortable, and yet insecure new middling class (travelling salesmen, saloon managers, and show girls: all hired hands in privately owned institutions of urban consumer capitalism); and centrally, the career of a young woman who "had no excellent home principles fixed upon her" (60) (a line which once again shows Dreiser's uncredited skill as a dead-pan ironist), who, far from suffering remorse or moral blame for enjoying sex outside marriage and inside adultery, actually grows in self-awareness and independence, and who, unmarried, unattached, successful in her career at the close of the narrative, seems poised to make something more and better of herself, "redeeming" in a transvalued sense of the word those very experiences unacceptably sordid and "unreal" in the eyes of gentility (including Howells) by becoming – we are led to believe it possible – a serious artist and serious person. The narrative problem was not so much to make this world and this process of growth credible (that was taken care of by Dreiser's monumental recollection of detail, the intonation, the slang, the style of bearing and gesture of this world, and most important, the emotional turmoils and petty dilemmas of "metropolitan success" and his own ambivalent struggles toward an expressive relation to this milieu), but to find an appropriate perspective upon it, a voice capable of speaking both from within, as an intimate and familiar, and from without, as a critical but sympathetic commentator. Another way of stating the problem is that Dreiser required a narrative form supple and flexible enough to allow the reader, in Lester Cohen's words, "to understand the social world from the standpoint of Dreiser's characters."[28]

The most significant method of achieving such a narrative, one of which Cohen alone among Dreiser's recent critics seems to have grasped the full importance, is the weight and presence he gives to "mental process," to consciousness, to how his world is experienced by his characters – how that fictive world is constituted by the modes of experience it contains, including that of the narrator.[29] Thus the critical importance of the *Under the Gaslight* episode, which we will not examine here in any detail – its importance for what it reveals about the subtle and complex interactions between theatricality and real life. That extended episode also clarifies what has been little noticed as a structural feature of the entire Chicago section: the triangulation of desire, the most prominent form of which is the intense male competition which drives Hurstwood – how, in short, Drouet mediates Hurstwood's desire for Carrie. Dreiser's great insight, which reaches an apogee during the play-within-a-play rendering of the performance at Avery Hall, concerns the imitativeness of desire – an insight also represented whenever Carrie employs her mirror to see herself as others see her, and to assume, as if in rehearsal, the look she believes others wish to see upon her face. Her mirror represents her self in the eyes of others:

> She looked in the mirror and pursed up her lips, accompanying it with a little toss of the head, as she had seen the railroad treasurer's daughter do. (78–9)

In a line deleted from the original manuscript, Dreiser wrote: "We are, after all, more passive than active, more mirrors than engines, and the origins of human action has neither yet been measured nor calculated" (78 Penn). Mirroring rather than initiating: this describes not only Carrie's condition but that of the entire milieu of

persons whose lives reflected more nakedly than that of the traditional respectable burgher families (missing from the book) the
daily fluxional workings of the marketplace – the sale of manufac-
tured objects in Drouet's case, of entertainment enhanced by social
prestige in Hurstwood's case, and in Carrie's as a show girl in New
York, the desired image of a desirable woman she mirrors back to
her insatiable audience (including, at the height of her success, the
audience for her published photograph – yet another mirror
[323–4]).

Imitation as the sign of the absent others who comprise the
social representivity of Dreiser's world is a major clue to the narrator's discursive method of address to the reader, one of his ways
of identifying the reader with a point of view both within and
without the conceptual world of the portrayed society. One device
by which he enforces this insight as both theme and action is his
voicing of the language of things, of objects, goods, commodities –
in Chapter 11, for example:

> Carrie was an apt student of fortune's ways – of fortune's super-
> ficialities. Seeing a thing, she would immediately set to inquiring
> how she would look, properly related to it [note the mirror implied
> here]. Be it known that this is not fine feeling, it is not wisdom. The
> greatest minds are not so afflicted; and on the contrary, the lowest
> order of mind is not so disturbed. Fine clothes to her were a vast
> persuasion; they spoke tenderly and Jesuistically for themselves.
> When she came within earshot of their pleading, desire in her bent
> a willing ear. The voice of the so-called inanimate! Who shall trans-
> late for us the language of the stones?
> "My dear," said the lace collar she secured from Partridge's, "I fit
> you beautifully; don't give me up."
> "Ah, such little feet," said the leather of the soft new shoes; "how
> effectively I cover them. What a pity they should ever want my aid."
> (75)

Translating the commodity appeal into a social *voice*, a voice which
speaks directly to Carrie in exactly the same way it speaks to all
who bend an ear – in short, a voice seducing Carrie to an act of
imitation disguised as an act of freedom, of autonomous purchase
(though in the following paragraph she struggles vainly with her
conscience about the price she pays with her body for the right to
feel autonomous in succumbing to the voice of goods) – by this

109

means Dreiser not only imagines a narrative equivalent to Marx's insight about the mystique of the commodity, but he makes the artifice of his own narrative method available to the reader, reveals his method as a sign of that "fine feeling" and "wisdom" the narrator and reader share as they witness Carrie's succumbing once more to a voice in her ear. The terms of the initial moral allegory, the melodrama initiated by the narrative voice in the opening paragraphs of the novel, continue in force: the perspective in which the reader distinguishes himself or herself from Carrie is sharpened even as he or she, learning that Carrie is not of "the lowest order of mind" but one of the new middle order of American, can also feel the persuasion – feel in order to place in a perspective of knowledge ("Be it known . . . ").

One of the fullest discursive commentaries on both the language of things and the adequacy of words appears in Chapter 12. His domestic life growing more dry, tense, threatening, Hurstwood invests greater "interest in Drouet's little shop-girl" which grows "in an almost evenly balanced proportion" to his unhappiness at home[30] (856). Subtle changes in Carrie add to her appeal. "She had an aptitude of the struggler who seeks emancipation," and under the tutelage of Mrs. Hale, "learns to distinguish between degrees of wealth" (85–6). Always making his own presence felt as the figure through whom we not only perceive Carrie but understand her mood or feeling or action precisely as a *present* state conditioned by the present situation, the narrator interjects what neither Carrie nor anyone else (until Ames appears later) can put into words: "She did not grow in knowledge so much as she awakened in desire" (86). The chapter narrates a crucial phase of an awakening *without* knowledge, an *ignorant* desire, and if the narrator's qualification escapes us (as it has most commentators), we miss the full dimension of the moment within Carrie's career of awakening self-consciousness.

An afternoon drive with Mrs. Hale to "look upon" the elegant new mansions on the North Shore Drive ends with a return along the same route at dusk.

> Lamps were beginning to burn with that mellow radiance which seems almost watery and translucent to the eye. There was a soft-

ness in the air which speaks with an infinite delicacy of feeling to the flesh as well as to the soul. Carrie felt that it was a lovely day. She was ripened by it in spirit for many suggestions. As they drove along the smooth pavement an occasional carriage passed. She saw one stop and the footman dismount, opening the door for a gentleman who seemed to be leisurely returning from some afternoon pleasure. Across the broad lawns, now first freshening into green, she saw lamps faintly glowing upon rich interiors. Now it was but a chair, now a table, now an ornate corner, which met her eye, but it appealed to her as almost nothing else could. Such childish fancies as she had had of fairy palaces and kingly quarters now came back. She imagined that across these richly carved entrance-ways, where the globed and crystalled lamps shone upon panelled doors set with stained and designed panes of glass, was neither care nor unsatisfied desire. She was perfectly certain that here was happiness. If she could but stroll up yon broad walk, cross that rich entrance-way, which to her was of the beauty of a jewel, and sweep in grace and luxury to possession and command – oh! how quickly would sadness flee; how, in an instant, would the heartache end. She gazed and gazed, wondering, delighting, longing, and all the while the siren voice of the unrestful was whispering in her ear. (86)

Except perhaps for the final image of the "siren voice," the entire extraordinary passage represents Carrie's point of view as pure narrative, the naive sincerity of her belief in the magical powers of the American bourgeois myth of "possession and command" present to her longing eyes as a poetry of *things,* of commodities disguised as transformative objects of desire: now a chair, now a table, now an ornate corner. Like the softness in the air these things *speak* to her; they possess a language, more articulate (as Poirier points out) than Carrie herself, who can respond only with a longing gaze across thresholds and into rich interiors. Trivial yet potent correlatives of an awakening of desire without benefit of a growth of knowledge, these commodities of magical speech betray the ignorance of her desire, the sorry little imitativeness of her imagination: "She was perfectly certain that here was happiness."

Dreiser makes us feel both the sincerity of her desire and the painful inadequacy of the objects to which it attaches itself – the pathos of her wish for happiness objectified by Shore Drive lawns and, as the chapter progresses, by the materiality of Hurstwood

111

himself. Hurstwood appears at her flat as she still luxuriates in the residue of longing aroused by the afternoon drive, and the narrator prepares for the powerful effect of the manager's glance upon her by commenting on Carrie's deficiencies of speech. "She was no talker. She could never arrange her thoughts in fluent order. It was always a matter of feeling with her, strong and deep. Each time [she had been in Hurstwood's presence] there had been no sentences of importance which she could relate" (88). At this point the narrator shifts his register of voice to continue the earlier discourse on words:

> People in general attach too much importance to words. They are under the illusion that talking effects great results. As a matter of fact, words are, as a rule, the shallowest portion of all the argument. They but dimly represent the surging feelings and desires which lie behind. When the distraction of the tongue is removed, the heart listens. (88)

Here commentary itself waxes sentimental as it rises to the tritest of synecdoches ("the heart listens"). How little do the actual words passing between Hurstwood and Carrie tell us what *really* passes between them!

But in continuing the discourse, now a more explicit commentary on the transpiring narrative event – the rather mindless talk between Carrie and Hurstwood – the narrator subtly recalls Carrie's experience in the carriage at dusk on the Shore Drive. It is as if Hurstwood's very person materialized the *feeling* of those rich interiors, the happiness they magically promised:

> In this conversation she heard, instead of his words, the voices of the things which he represented. How suave was the counsel of his appearance! How feelingly did his superior state speak for itself! The growing desire he felt for her lay upon her spirit as a gentle hand. She did not need to tremble at all, because it was invisible; she did not need to worry over what other people would say – what she herself would say – because it had no tangibility. She was being pleaded with, persuaded, led into denying old rights and assuming new ones, and yet there were no words to prove it. Such conversation as was indulged in held the same relationships to the actual mental enactments of the twain that the low music of the orchestra does to the dramatic incident which it is used to cover. (88–9)

112

The paragraph is remarkable for its return to an effective indirect discourse which reconstructs, not in their own language but in a figurative language addressed to the reader, the subtle exchange of inarticulate but palpable meanings between Carrie and Hurstwood. Rather than conversation as such the narrator represents inner experience, "the actual mental enactments of the twain," through a figure of theatricality (the reference in the final sentence uncannily anticipates the musical accompaniment of silent cinema melodramas, which were about to appear in city nickelodeons shortly after the novel appeared): the conversational words bear the same relation to inner feeling as the music of the theatre orchestra does to "dramatic incident."

But the inner life represented, or more accurately, translated from feelings analogous to music into words that give the feelings a certain precision, is an intersubjectivity quite concretely represented as social, as a discourse on property rights and legal evidence. "Denying old rights and assuming new ones" alludes to the triangulation within which Carrie and Hurstwood make all their moves, conscious of Drouet without having to name him – which makes it possible for Carrie to overlook the objective social fact of her virtual contractual surrender of "rights" to the man who pays the bills: another note in the narrative voice by which Dreiser socializes the evolving perspective in which Carrie's desires and her realities can be seen in dialectical tension.

The opening line of the paragraph underscores the more general social vision of the total narrative perspective – that the things which the narrator translates are *representative* things. Carrie *feels* Hurstwood as representative of "things," feels him (unable to put this into words, and thus saved from the social recognitions by which the reader is able to refine a closeness/distance relation to her predicament) as metonymically what he possesses, his *being* identical with the things he owns (for the time being, at least; his wife is already at work readjusting the property rights), identified with what, which means also *who*, he represents: the absent others who constitute his historical class – the class of bourgeois retainers which in the end cannot save him from the fate already implicit as the nightmare underside (realized in the theft scene) of his particular form of managerial success.

In the original manuscript Dreiser followed this remarkably precise and powerful passage with a paragraph of didactic explanation, which included the following account of his conceptual intention:

> The forces which regulate two individuals of the character of Carrie and Hurstwood are as strange and as subtle as described. We have been writing our novels and our philosophies without sufficiently emphasizing them – we have been neglecting to set forth what all men must know and feel about these things before a true and natural life may be led. *We must understand that not we, but the things of which we are the evidence, are the realities* [emphasis supplied]. (119 Penn)

This can well be read to mean evidence of "the great forces of nature" – the desires for sex, for warmth, for male domination, for victory over another male – but it can also be read, consistent with readings I have suggested so far, as saying that reality is the totality of our relations, possessions, desires, all that comprise us as selves and that we can be said to represent, as they represent us. In the first reading, the one likely to be endorsed by Poirier, Dreiser diminishes the human before "the great forces"; the second has him recognizing the historical and social character of humankind – the representivity which makes our reality, as Brecht and Emerson both understood, always more than we ourselves can know or in any single instance enact.

5

If we are not, in our illusion of autonomy, of being free agents in the marketplaces of desire, the reality but rather what we represent, our natural and social histories, then what place does Dreiser's narrative method allow for heroic action? What opportunities exist for the knowledge Ames encourages Carrie to value above all else to change her life in practical, purposeful ways? *Sister Carrie* leaves its major questions hanging inconclusively, rocking in the wind, we might say – questions about the dialectic between freedom and necessity, about the sources of identity and self-presence within social relations.[31]

Denying redemption, the novel fails as social reassurance, and in this lies much of its negative, subversive power. It alters the perspective in which Carrie, a representative figure, only gets worse, and would have us believe at the end that she may yet better herself in a transvalued moral order. Hope for Carrie seems prefigured in the hope Dreiser the author realized for himself, not just in the writing of the book but in the invention of a narrative-discursive voice whose significance may lie in its giving first expression in American fiction to a modernist version of the self-made artist-as-hero. Dreiser's presence in *Sister Carrie* is not merely to tell the tale but to tell it as his own experience, and to persuade his readers that only such a telling can set before them the inaudible realities of the new America — realities it took the brother of Paul Dresser and the friend of H. L. Mencken to know from both sides, inside and out.[32]

NOTES

1. See the documents on "publication" and the "legend" gathered in Donald Pizer, ed., *Sister Carrie* (New York: Norton, 1970), pp. 433–470; all page references in the text are to this edition of the novel. I have found especially valuable for their integration of biographical and historical data with critical insight Ellen Moers, *Two Dreisers* (New York: Viking, 1969), especially parts 1–3; and Donald Pizer, *The Novels of Theodore Dreiser; A Critical Study* (Minneapolis: University of Minnesota Press, 1976), especially pp. 31–95. Two useful biographical studies are W. A. Swanberg, *Dreiser* (New York: Scribners, 1969), and Richard Lingeman, *Theodore Dreiser: At the Gates of the City, 1871–1907* (New York: Putnam, 1986).

2. I have in mind, in the order of my allusions to their themes, recent essays or chapters by Walter Benn Michaels, *The Gold Standard and the Logic of Naturalism* (Berkeley: University of California Press, 1987), chapter 1; Amy Kaplan, *The Social Construction of American Realism* (Chicago: University of Chicago Press, 1988), chapters 5–6; Sandy Petry, "The Language of Realism, The Language of False Consciousness: A Reading of Sister Carrie," *Novel* 10 (Winter 1977): 101–13; and the exchange between Petry and Ellen Moers, "Critical Exchange: Dreiser's Wisdom or Stylistic Discontinuities?" *Novel* 11 (Fall 1977): 63–9. The reference to "linguistic junk" is from Frederic Jam-

eson's few remarks on Dreiser in *The Political Unconscious* (Ithaca: Cornell University Press, 1981), p. 159, which include the somewhat inscrutable obiter dictum: "The axiological paradox about Dreiser – he is best at his worst . . . " Sandy Petry proposes a compelling but finally unpersuasive explanation, that the text of *Sister Carrie* can be likened to a battleground between discontinuous styles – the bad sentimentality of popular romance, and the good objective realism of the best dialogue and description. The former represents the "false consciousness" Dreiser wants to exorcise by exaggerating its irrelevance and parodying its destructive illusions, while the latter represents a Hemingway-like liberating honesty through which the illusions of consumer capitalism can be seen for what they are. There is much to recommend this view, but in the end it suffers from its own ingenuity and simplification. To divide Dreiser's writing in *Sister Carrie* into two competing styles is one mistake – the verbal discontinuities are multiple; to see the variety of styles as separable from each other is another – rare is the passage entirely free of authorial editorializing; and to valorize the Hemingway laconism as a novelistic style is yet another. See Gerard Genette's remarks in *Figures of Literary Discourse* (New York: Columbia University Press, 1982), p. 143, on the novelistic liabilities of the Hammett–Hemingway "purity" of narrative style. Finally, to see Dreiser as an implacable foe of consumer capitalism misses the positive value the novel sets upon Carrie's "false consciousness," for the things (commodities) which speak to her awaken precisely those desires commodity culture in the end cannot satisfy, thus advancing the process of her awakening. Dreiser's relation to the world he depicts is more ambiguous and dialectical than Petry allows. I am indebted in my thinking about Dreiser's view of the positive elements within consumerism to a brilliant unpublished paper by James Livingston, "Form, Self, History: *Sister Carrie's* Absent Causes." Professor Livingston also sees the novel as a battleground – between the generic modes of "realism" and "romance" – a provocative historicizing and periodizing argument too rich to summarize here (see note 25). Other recent works which propose useful reinterpretations of the novel in its history are Rachel Bowlby, *Just Looking* (New York: Methuen, 1985); Philip Fisher, *Hard Facts: Setting and Form in the American Novel* (New York: Oxford University Press, 1985); June Howard, *Form and History in American Literary Naturalism* (Chapel Hill: University of North Carolina Press, 1985); and Robert Shulman, *Social Criticism in Nineteenth-Century American Fiction* (Columbia: University of Missouri Press, 1987).

3. F. O. Matthiessen, *Theodore Dreiser* (New York: William Sloane Associates, 1951), p. 60. Matthiessen attributed Dreiser's method to his reading of Balzac. Writing in 1922 about his first encounter with Balzac's works in 1894 – "It was for me a literary revolution" – Dreiser noted that the French author's "grand and somewhat pompous philosophical deductions, his easy and offhand disposition of all manner of critical, social, political, historical, religious problems, the manner in which he assumed as by right of genius intimate and irrefutable knowledge of all subjects, fascinated and captured me as the true method of the seer and the genius" (Pizer, ed., *Sister Carrie*, p. 402). The suggestion is strong that his reading of Balzac in this spirit contributed in a major way to the eclectic narrative method he devised for his own first novel in 1900.

4. See especially Fisher, *Hard Facts,* chapter 3, "The Life History of Objects: The Naturalist Novel and the City."

5. Percy Lubbock, *The Craft of Fiction* (New York: Viking, 1957), pp. 251–64. Lubbock's concern in these pages with "point of view – the question of the relation in which the narrator stands to the story" (p. 251) has, I believe, limited relevance to the characteristic interfusion by Dreiser (as by Balzac) of "reflective summary of events" (the Jamesian "picture"), the self-enactment of the events of the story ("scene"), and what Seymour Chatman, in *Story and Discourse: Narrative Structure in Fiction and Film* (Ithaca: Cornell University Press, 1978), p. 228, describes as "commentary" which can take the form of "an entire gamut of speech acts."

6. Richard Poirier, *A World Elsewhere: The Place of Style in American Literature* (New York: Oxford University Press, 1966), p. 238. Subsequent page references in the text (WE) refer to this edition.

7. William L. Phillips, "The Imagery of Dreiser's Novels," *PMLA* 78 (December 1963): 572–5; reprinted in Pizer, ed., *Sister Carrie*, pp. 551–8. Also see Pizer on the novel's symbolism, *Novels of Theodore Dreiser,* pp. 31–95, and Fisher on its patterns of space and movement, *Hard Facts,* pp. 153–78.

8. Julian Markels, "Dreiser and the Plotting of Inarticulate Experience," *The Massachusetts Review* 2 (Spring 1961): 431–48; reprinted in Pizer, ed., *Sister Carrie,* p. 529.

9. *Ibid.*, p. 530.

10. Leo Bersani, *A Future for Astyanax: Character and Desire in Literature* (Boston: Little, Brown, 1976), p. 53. "Behavior in realistic fiction is continuously expressive of character. Apparently random incidents carry messages about personality; and the world is thus at least struc-

turally congenial to character, in the sense that it is constantly propos-
ing to our intelligence objects and events which contain human
desires, which give to them an intelligible form." The danger confronted by nineteenth-century realists such as Balzac, Bersani argues,
is "a diffusion of meaning" threatened by excessive desire. "In a
novelistic universe deprived of some governing pattern of significance, all events may be equally important" (p. 52). Although not
directly cogent to the issue of the narrator's role in *Sister Carrie*,
Michaels's debate with Bersani over desire, character, and novelistic
form does bear on the question; see Michaels, *Gold Standard*, pp. 46–
54. Fisher's characterization of Dreiser's characters as possessing a
"self in anticipation" (p. 157) rather than one to which they might be
"true" (p. 140) seems to follow from Poirier's observation about the
"negligible" role of social selves in *Sister Carrie* compared to the world
of articulate "objects."

11. William J. Handy, "A Re-Examination of Dreiser's *Sister Carrie*," *Texas
Studies in Literature and Language* (Autumn 1959): 380–9; reprinted
in Pizer, ed., *Sister Carrie*, p. 522: subsequent page references in the
text (H) are to the latter edition. It is worth saying at this point that
inserting himself as a "looming presence" was surely a deliberate
choice (though not without buried psychic motives: see note 12). His
competence in creating central point of view characters and in em-
ploying indirect discourse is perfectly evident in two stories written
before *Sister Carrie*, "Nigger Jeff" and "McEwen of the Shining Slave
Makers." See Howard, *Form and History*, pp. 106–7.

12. The imaginative rapport between Dreiser and Carrie may well be the
chief issue in the problem of the narrator's relation to his materials –
one which I do my best to scant in this essay; it is simply too large, too
dangerous for a brief discussion. Moers, *Two Dreisers*, is especially
good on Dreiser's use of family experiences in the novel and suggests
his ambivalence. The best insights into the narrative effects of Dreiser's
doubling himself in his portrayal of Carrie as self-punishment for his
own "wild dreams of some far-off supremacy" are in Robert Penn
Warren, *Homage to Theodore Dreiser* (New York: Random House,
1971); Warren writes (p. 331) that "*Sister Carrie* appears as the projection of his own secret conflict and self-scrutiny; perhaps not the
projection of them, but the means by which he discovered them at
all." A full account of the sources of Dreiser's alternating closeness to
and distance from Carrie must take the particular Dreiserian psychosis
of his early career into account.

13. Moers, *Two Dreisers*, contains an excellent, vivid account of Dreiser's

own involvements with the emerging metropolitan mass culture, his relations with his brother Paul, who epitomized "metropolitan celebrity," and his own experience as a writer of magazine fiction. The essays in Richard W. Fox and T. J. Lears, eds., *The Culture of Consumption* (New York: Pantheon, 1983) contain relevant materials: see especially Christopher Wilson, "The Rhetoric of Consumption: Mass-Market Magazines and the Demise of the Gentle Reader, 1880–1920," pp. 39–64.

14. Livingston's unpublished essay (see note 2) offers a valuable perspective on the political economy of the era represented by the novel. Other relevant works on cultural change and political economy in the period include Lewis Erenberg, *Steppin' Out: New York Nightlife and the Transformation of American Culture, 1890–1930* (Chicago: University of Chicago Press, 1981); T. J. Lears, *No Place of Grace: Antimodernism and the Transformation of American Culture, 1880–1920* (New York: Pantheon, 1981); William R. Leach, "Transformations in a Culture of Consumption: Women and Department Stores, 1890–1925," *Journal of American History* 71 (1984): 319–42; Kathy Peiss, *Cheap Amusements: Working Women and Leisure in Turn of the Century New York* (Philadelphia: Temple University Press, 1986); Martin Sklar, *The Corporate Reconstruction of American Capitalism, 1890–1916* (Cambridge University Press, 1988); Warren Susman, "'Personality' and the Making of Twentieth Century Culture," in *Culture as History: The Transformation of American Society in the Twentieth Century* (New York: Pantheon, 1984), pp. 271–85; and William Appleman Williams, *The Contours of American History* (Cleveland: World Publishing Co., 1961).

15. Genette, *Figures*, pp. 138, 139, 140, 142.

16. Donald Pizer makes the important point that "The underlying function of many of Dreiser's philosophical comments . . . is less to establish a particular abstract truth which should guide our rational consideration of an incident or character than to elicit from us a sentiment which aids Dreiser fictionally at the moment in question" (Pizer, *Novels of Theodore Dreiser*, p. 87). The case might be made even more strongly that virtually all his apparent digressions, when read with an ear to Dreiser's irony, have local before universal applications.

17. For an *almost* convincing account of how conventional a middle-brow sentimental-seduction novel *Sister Carrie* is, see Leslie Fiedler, *Love and Death in the American Novel* (New York: Criterion Books, 1960), pp. 241–8. See also Sheldon N. Grebstein, "Dreiser's Victorian Vamp," *Midcontinent American Studies Journal* 4 (Spring 1963): 3–12; reprinted in Pizer, ed., *Sister Carrie*, pp. 541–51, for a useful examina-

tion of Dreiser's making of Carrie into a conventional "love goddess," with "ambivalent sophistication and naivete" (p. 551).

18. John J. McDermott, ed., *William James: A Comprehensive Edition* (New York: Random House, 1967), "Does 'Consciousness' Exist?" pp. 169–83, and "The Notion of Consciousness," pp. 184–93.

19. See, for example, the ironic play on "I know" and "I don't know" in the tense meeting of Carrie and Hurstwood after he has unfolded his proposition to take her away from Drouet, pp. 149–50.

20. Leon Edel, ed., *Henry James: The Art of the Novel* (New York: Vintage, 1956), p. 57.

21. *Ibid.*, p. 54.

22. Olaf Hansen, ed., *The Radical Will: Randolph Bourne, Selected Writings, 1911–1918* (New York: Urizen Books, 1977), "Theodore Dreiser," pp. 459–61.

23. Quoted in Jack Saltzman, ed., *Theodore Dreiser: The Critical Reception* (New York: David Lewis, 1972), p. 53, from the Akron [Ohio] *Journal*, November 30, 1907.

24. See note 14.

25. Livingston argues that Dreiser does just this – leaps over Howells and Mark Twain to the American romancers, particularly Hawthorne of *The Blithedale Romance* and Melville of *The Confidence Man*, both highly theatricalized texts, seeking a "romance" mode by which he might open "realism" to desire and the provisionality of theatrical identities as modes of self-realization. An allusion to Hawthorne's *Twice-Told Tales* in the original manuscript of *Sister Carrie* in connection with "that mingled atmosphere of life and mummery" (176 Penn) in the backstage scene before the performance of *Under the Gaslight* lends some weight to Livingston's argument, which at the least encourages us to reconsider sources in American romantic writing for Dreiser's revisions of realistic narrative to allow a freer discursive role for the narrator's voice – and for the narrator's own discharge of desire as expression of his own self-realization.

26. See note 14.

27. Wai-Chee Dimock, "The Economy of Pain: The Case of Howells," *Raritan Review* 9 (Spring 1990): 99–119.

28. Lester H. Cohen, "Locating One's Self: The Problematics of Dreiser's Social World," *Modern Fiction Studies* 23 (Autumn 1977): 358. Professor Cohen shows that Dreiser's ideas about social and personal identity parallel many of the key concepts in turn-of-the-century social theory in Europe and America.

29. The correspondence between Dreiser's narrator's effort to establish a

dialogic relation with the assumed reader and George Herbert Mead's theory of "sociality" is quite striking. For example, Mead writes: "The social organization of perspectives arises through the individual's taking the role of the other within a social act whose varied phases are in some sense present in his organism. When, therefore, he has within the social act stimulated himself to act as the other, he has aroused the beginnings of the act of the other in its relationship to his own act and the whole process." Mead calls this process of undertaking to live and act imaginatively in the role of the other the "phase of sociality" – quite similar to what Dreiser imagines as the effect of his narrative upon his reader, which corresponds to the act his narrator performs in relation to the characters in his story. Charles W. Morris, ed., *Works of George Herbert Mead, Volume 3: The Philosophy of the Act* (Chicago: University of Chicago Press, 1938), p. 610.

30. Dreiser's apparent pun on "interest," and the not-so-buried allusion to a balance sheet, suggest not only the invasion of Hurstwood's consciousness by the rhetoric of cash nexus, not only the universally held assumption within his milieu of the naturalness of property rights in women inside and outside arrangements sanctified by legal marriage, but also, as unconscious anticipation, his actual investment into his desired property claim over Carrie of the hard cash (including the soft paper bills) which he steals from his employers (as he in effect steals by abduction Drouet's property in Carrie). That act of theft in the interest of acquiring a movable property he wishes to remove from circulation (Carrie) ironically turns against him and initiates his downward slide in two senses: (1) the theft of cash virtually disqualifies him for access to credit, more potent than cash in the new "monetary regime," as Livingston puts it, establishing itself in the 1890s; and (2) he fails to anticipate that Carrie might develop an "interest" in *herself* as an instrument of value, as she indeed becomes "worth" not only the rolls of paper cash which burst in her purse but the "credit" of her name and pictures upon which she acquires shelter without payment at the Waldorf, just as Hurstwood reaches the point of "What's the use?"

31. See Kaplan's suggestive remark (*Social Construction*, p. 160) that "Realistic novels have trouble ending because they pose problems they cannot solve, problems that stem from their very attempt to imagine and contain social change." One major obstacle to a satisfactory ending for *Sister Carrie* is the relative weakness of plot. What complication remains to be resolved? Dreiser invented a voice – does it reappear in the narrative persona of Henry Miller? – dangerous to narrative for its

Notes on Contributors

Barbara Hochman teaches in the Department of English and American Literature at Tel Aviv University. She is the author of *The Art of Frank Norris, Storyteller* (1988) and of essays on Dreiser and Edith Wharton. She is currently working on a book that examines changing conditions of authorship as reflected in turn-of-the-century American fiction.

Richard Lehan, Professor of English at the University of California, Los Angeles, is the author of *Theodore Dreiser: His World and His Novels* (1969). His other works include *F. Scott Fitzgerald and the Craft of Fiction* (1966), *A Dangerous Crossing: French Literary Existentialism and the Modern American Novel* (1973), and *The Great Gatsby: The Limits of Wonder* (1990).

Donald Pizer is Pierce Butler Professor of English at Tulane University. Among his books on Dreiser are *The Novels of Theodore Dreiser: A Critical Study* (1976), *Theodore Dreiser: A Primary and Secondary Bibliography,* with Richard Dowell and Frederic Rusch (1975), *Theodore Dreiser: A Selection of Uncollected Prose* (1977), *Critical Essays on Theodore Dreiser* (1981), and editions of *Sister Carrie* (1970) and *Jennie Gerhardt* (1989). He has also published studies of Hamlin Garland, Frank Norris, and John Dos Passos.

Thomas P. Riggio, Professor of English at the University of Connecticut, Storrs, is general editor of the Pennsylvania Edition of Dreiser's work. In addition to a number of essays on Dreiser, he has edited Dreiser's *American Diaries, 1902–1926* (1982) and *Dreiser-Mencken Letters: The Correspondence of Theodore Dreiser and H. L.*

Mencken, 1907–1945 (1986). He has also written on, among others, Mencken, Poe, Harriet Beecher Stowe, Isaac Bashevis Singer, and Mark Twain.

Alan Trachtenberg is Neil Gray, Jr. Professor of English and American Studies at Yale University. His books include *Brooklyn Bridge: Fact and Symbol* (1965), *The Incorporation of America: Culture and Society in the Gilded Age* (1982), and *Reading American Photographs: Images as History, Mathew Brady to Walker Evans* (1989). He has also edited a number of books dealing with American literature and American photography.

Selected Bibliography

Ahnebrink, Lars. "Dreiser's *Sister Carrie* and Balzac." *Symposium* 7 (November 1953): 306–22.

Bowlby, Rachel. "Starring: Dreiser's *Sister Carrie,*" in *Just Looking: Consumer Culture in Dreiser, Gissing, and Zola*. New York: Methuen, 1985.

Brennan, Stephen C. "*Sister Carrie* and the Tolstoyan Artist." *Research Studies* 47 (March 1979): 1–16.

"The Two Endings of *Sister Carrie*." *Studies in American Fiction* 16 (Spring 1988): 13–26.

Burgan, Mary A. "*Sister Carrie* and the Pathos of Naturalism." *Criticism* 15 (Fall 1973): 336–49.

Davidson, Cathy N. and Arnold E. "Carrie's Sisters: The Popular Stereotypes for Dreiser's Heroines." *Modern Fiction Studies* 23 (Autumn 1977): 395–407.

Dreiser, Helen. *My Life with Dreiser*. Cleveland: World, 1951.

Dudley, Dorothy. *Forgotten Frontiers: Dreiser and the Land of the Free*. New York: Harrison Smith, 1932.

Elias, Robert H. *Theodore Dreiser: Apostle of Nature*. Rev ed., Ithaca: Cornell University Press, 1970.

ed. *Letters of Theodore Dreiser*. 3 vols. Philadelphia: University of Pennsylvania Press, 1959.

Fisher, Philip. "The Life History of Objects: The Naturalist Novel and the City," in *Hard Facts: Setting and Form in the American Novel*. New York: Oxford University Press, 1985.

Freedman, William A. "A Look at Dreiser as Artist: The Motif of Circularity in *Sister Carrie*." *Modern Fiction Studies* 8 (Winter 1962–63): 384–92.

Gelfant, Blanche H. "Theodore Dreiser: The Portrait Novel," in *The American City Novel*. Norman: University of Oklahoma Press, 1954.

Gerber, Philip H. *Theodore Dreiser*. New York: Twayne, 1964.

Handy, William J. "A Re-Examination of Dreiser's *Sister Carrie*." *Texas Studies in Literature and Language* 1 (Autumn 1959): 380–9.

Kaplan, Amy. "The Sentimental Revolt of *Sister Carrie,*" in *The Social Construction of American Realism.* Chicago: University of Chicago Press, 1988.

Katope, Christopher. "*Sister Carrie* and Spencer's *First Principles.*" *American Literature* 41 (March 1969): 64–75.

Kazin, Alfred, and Shapiro, Charles, eds. *The Stature of Theodore Dreiser.* Bloomington: Indiana University Press, 1955.

Lehan, Richard. *Theodore Dreiser: His World and His Novels.* Carbondale: Southern Illinois University Press, 1969.

Lingeman, Richard. *Theodore Dreiser: At the Gates of the City, 1871–1907.* New York: Putnam's, 1986.

Theodore Dreiser: An American Journey, 1908–1945. New York: Putnam's, 1990.

Lydenberg, John, ed. *Dreiser: A Collection of Critical Essays.* Englewood Cliffs, N. J.: Prentice-Hall, 1971.

Lynn, Kenneth. "Introduction" to *Sister Carrie.* New York: Holt, Rinehart, Winston, 1957.

Markels, Julian. "Dreiser and the Plotting of Inarticulate Experience." *Massachusetts Review* 2 (Spring 1961): 431–8.

Matthiessen, F. O. *Theodore Dreiser.* New York: Sloane, 1951.

Mencken, H. L. "Theodore Dreiser." *A Book of Prefaces.* New York: Knopf, 1917.

Michaels, Walter Benn. "*Sister Carrie's* Popular Economy," in *The Gold Standard and the Logic of Naturalism.* Berkeley: University of California Press, 1987.

Moers, Ellen. "The Finesse of Dreiser." *American Scholar* 33 (Winter 1963–64): 109–44.

Two Dreisers. New York: Viking, 1969.

Phillips, William L. "The Imagery of Dreiser's Novels." *PMLA* 78 (December 1963): 572–85.

Petrey, Sandy. "The Language of Realism, The Language of False Consciousness: A Reading of *Sister Carrie.*" *Novel* 10 (Winter 1977): 101–13.

Pizer, Donald. *Realism and Naturalism in Nineteenth-Century American Literature.* Rev ed., Carbondale: Southern Illinois University Press, 1984.

The Novels of Theodore Dreiser: A Critical Study. Minneapolis: University of Minnesota Press, 1976.

ed. *Critical Essays on Theodore Dreiser.* Boston: G. K. Hall, 1981.

Dowell, Richard W., and Rusch, Frederic E. *Theodore Dreiser: A Primary and Secondary Bibliography.* Boston: G. K. Hall, 1975.

Poirier, Richard. "Panoramic Environment and the Anonymity of the Self," in *A World Elsewhere: The Place of Style in American Literature.* New York: Oxford University Press, 1966.

Riggio, Thomas P., ed. *Dreiser–Mencken Letters: The Correspondence of The-*

odore Dreiser and H. L. Mencken, 1907–1945. Philadelphia: University of Pennsylvania Press, 1986.

Salzman, Jack, ed. *Theodore Dreiser: The Critical Reception.* New York: David Lewis, 1972.

"The Publication of *Sister Carrie:* Fact and Fiction." *Library Chronicle* of the University of Pennsylvania Library 44 (Spring 1979): 7–26.

Sherman, Stuart P. "The Naturalism of Mr. Dreiser." *Nation* 101 (December 2, 1915): 648–50.

Shulman, Robert. "Dreiser and the Dynamics of American Capitalism," in *Social Criticism and Nineteenth-Century American Fictions.* Columbia: University of Missouri Press, 1987.

Swanberg, W. A. *Dreiser.* New York: Scribners, 1965.

Trilling, Lionel. "Reality in America," in *The Liberal Imagination.* New York: Viking, 1950.

Walcutt, Charles C. *American Literary Naturalism, A Divided Stream.* Minneapolis: University of Minnesota Press, 1956.

Warren, Robert Penn. *Homage to Theodore Dreiser. . .* New York: Random House, 1971.

West, James L. W. III. *"Sister Carrie:* Manuscript to Print," in *Sister Carrie, the Pennsylvania Edition,* ed. John C. Berkey et al. Philadelphia: University of Pennsylvania Press, 1981.

A Sister Carrie Portfolio. Charlottesville: University Press of Virginia, 1985.

Witemeyer, Hugh. "Gaslight and Magic Lamp in *Sister Carrie." PMLA* 86 (March 1971): 236–40.